✧ *Companions for the Journey* ✧

Praying with
Francis Assisi

✧ *Companions for the Journey* ✧

Praying with Francis Assisi

by
Joseph Stoutzenberger
and
John Bohrer

theWORD
among us®

To our companions for the journey:

✧   *Terry, Maurice, Dwight, Richard, and Joe*   ✧
JDB

✧   *Mom and Dad*   ✧
JMS

The acknowledgments continue on page 103.

Printed in the United States of America

ISBN 0-932085-86-5

✧ Contents ✧

✧ Foreword ✧

Companions for the Journey

Just as food is required for human life, so are companions. Indeed, the word *companions* comes from two Latin words: *com,* meaning "with," and *panis,* meaning "bread." Companions nourish our heart, mind, soul, and body. They are also the people with whom we can celebrate the sharing of bread.

Perhaps the most touching stories in the Bible are about companionship: the Last Supper, the wedding feast at Cana, the sharing of the loaves and the fishes, and Jesus breaking bread with the disciples on the road to Emmaus. Each incident of companionship with Jesus revealed more about his mercy, love, wisdom, suffering, and hope. When Jesus went to pray in the Garden of Olives, he craved the companionship of the Apostles. They let him down. But God sent the Spirit to inflame the hearts of the Apostles, and they became faithful companions to Jesus and to each other.

Throughout history, other faithful companions have followed Jesus and the Apostles. These saints and mystics have also taken the journey from conversion, through suffering, to resurrection. Just as they were inspired by the holy people who went before them, so too may you take them as your companions as you walk on your spiritual journey.

The Companions for the Journey series is a response to the spiritual hunger of Christians. This series makes available the rich spiritual teachings of mystics and guides whose wisdom can help us on our pilgrimage. As you complete the last meditation in each volume, it is hoped that you will feel supported, challenged, and affirmed by a soul-companion on your spiritual journey.

The spiritual hunger that has emerged over the last twenty years is a great sign of renewal in Christian life. People fill retreat programs and workshops on topics in spirituality. The demand for spiritual directors exceeds the number available. Interest in the lives and writings of saints and mystics is increasing as people search for models of whole and holy Christian life.

Praying with the Saints

Praying with Francis of Assisi is more than just a book about Francis' spirituality. This book seeks to engage you in praying in the way that Francis did about issues and themes that were central to his experience. Each meditation can enlighten your understanding of his revelations and lead you to reflect on your own experience.

The goal of *Praying with Francis of Assisi* is that you will discover his wonderfully alive spirituality and integrate his spirit and wisdom into your relationship with God, with your brothers and sisters, and with your own heart and mind.

Suggestions for Praying with Francis

Meet Francis, a caring companion for your pilgrimage, by reading the Introduction, which begins on page 13. It provides a brief biography of Francis and an outline of his dramatic conversion. The major themes of his spirituality are also highlighted.

Once you meet Francis, you will be ready to pray with him and to encounter God, Mother Earth, his human sisters and brothers, and yourself in new and wonderful ways. To help your prayer, here are some suggestions that have been part of the tradition of Christian spirituality:

Create a sacred space. Jesus said, "When you pray, go to your private room, shut yourself in, and so pray to your God who is in that secret place, and your God who sees all that is done in secret will reward you" (Matthew 6:5–6). Solitary prayer is best done in a place where you can have privacy and silence, both of which can be luxuries in the lives of busy people. If privacy and silence are not possible, create a quiet, safe place within yourself, perhaps while riding to and from work, while sitting in line at the dentist's office, or while waiting for someone. Do the best you can, knowing that a loving God is present everywhere. Whether the meditations in this book are used for solitary prayer or with a group, try to create a prayerful mood with candles, meditative music, a cross, an image of Mary, or an icon of Francis.

Open yourself to the power of prayer. Every human experience has a religious dimension. All of life is suffused with God's presence. So remind yourself that God is present as you begin your period of prayer. Do not worry about distractions. If something keeps intruding during your prayer, spend some time talking with God about it. Be flexible because God's Spirit blows where it will.

Prayer can open your mind and widen your vision. Be open to new ways of seeing God, people, and yourself. As you open yourself to the Spirit of God, different emotions are evoked, such as sadness from tender memories, or joy from a celebration recalled. Our emotions are messages from God that can tell us much about our spiritual quest. Also, prayer strengthens our will to act. Through prayer, God can touch our will and empower us to live according to what we know is true.

Finally, many of the meditations in this book will call you to employ your memories, your imagination, and the circumstances of your life as subjects for prayer. The great mystics and saints realized that they had to use all of their resources to know God better. Indeed, God speaks to us continually and touches us constantly. We must learn to listen and feel with all the means that God gave us.

Come to prayer with an open mind, heart, and will.

Preview each meditation before beginning. Spend a few moments previewing the readings and especially the reflection activities. Several reflection activities are given in each meditation because different styles of prayer appeal to different personalities or personal needs. **Note that each meditation has more reflection activities than can be done during one prayer period. Therefore, select only one or two reflection activities each time you use a meditation. Do not feel compelled to complete all of the reflection activities.**

Read meditatively. After you have placed yourself in God's presence, the meditations offer you a story about Francis and a reading from his writings. Take your time reading. If a particular phrase touches you, stay with it.

Use the reflections. Following the readings is a short reflection in commentary form meant to give perspective to the readings. Then you will be offered several ways of meditating on the readings and the theme of the prayer. You may be familiar with the different methods of meditating, but in case you are not, they are described briefly here:

✦ *Repeated short prayer or prayer word:* One means of focusing your prayer is to use a prayer word. It may be a single word or a short phrase taken from the readings or from the Scriptures. For example, a prayer word for a meditation on courage might be "I go before you" or "trust." Repeated slowly in harmony with your breathing, the prayer word helps you center your heart and mind on one action or attribute of God.

✦ *Lectio divina:* This type of meditation is "divine studying," a concentrated reflection on the word of God or the wisdom of a spiritual writer. Most often in *lectio divina* you will be invited to read one of the passages several times and then concentrate on one or two sentences, pondering their meaning for you and their effect on you. *Lectio divina* commonly ends with formulation of a resolution.

✦ *Guided meditation:* In this type of meditation, our imagination helps us consider alternative actions and likely consequences. Our imaginations help us experience new ways of seeing God, our neighbors, ourselves, and nature. When Jesus told his followers parables and stories, he engaged their imagination. In this book you will be asked to follow a guided meditation.

One way of doing a guided meditation is to read the scene or story several times until you know the outline and can recall it when you enter into reflection. Or prior to your prayer time, you may wish to record the meditation on a tape recorder. If so, remember to allow pauses for reflection between phrases and to speak with a slow, peaceful pace and tone. Then during prayer, when you have finished the readings and the reflection commentary, you can turn on your recording of the meditation and be led through it. If you find your own voice too distracting, ask a friend to make the tape for you.

✦ *Examen of consciousness:* The reflections often will ask you to examine how God has been speaking to you in your past and present experience—in other words, the reflections will ask you to examine your awareness of God's presence in your life.

✦ *Journal writing:* Writing is a process of discovery. If you write for any length of time, stating honestly what is on your mind and in your heart, you will unearth much about who you are, how you stand with your God, what deep longings reside in your soul, and more. In some of the reflections you may be asked to write a dialog with Jesus or someone else. If you have never used writing as a means of meditation, try it. Reserve a special notebook for your journal writing. If desired, you can go back to your entries at a future time for an examen of consciousness.

✦ *Action:* Occasionally, a reflection may suggest singing a favorite hymn, going out for a walk, or undertaking some other physical activity. Actions can be meaningful forms of prayer.

Using the Meditations for Family or Group Prayer

If you wish to use the meditations for family or community prayer, these suggestions may be of help:

✦ Read the theme to the group. Call the group into the presence of God, using the short opening prayer. Invite one or two participants to read one or both of the readings. If you use both readings, observe the pause between them.

✦ The reflection commentary may be used as a reading, or it can be deleted, depending on the needs and interests of the group.

✦ Select one of the reflection activities for your group. Allow sufficient time for your group to reflect, to do a centering prayer or prayer word, to accomplish a studying prayer (*lectio divina*), or to finish an examen of consciousness. Depending on the group and the amount of available time, you may want to invite the participants to share their reflections, responses, or petitions with the group.

✦ Reading the passage from the Scriptures may serve as a summary of the meditation.

✦ If a formulated prayer or a psalm is given as a closing, it may be recited by the entire group. Or you may ask participants to offer their own prayers for the closing.

Now you are ready to pray with Francis of Assisi, a delightful and challenging companion on this stage of your spiritual journey. For centuries, Francis has been a welcomed guide and supportive friend for people seeking a closer relationship with God. It is hoped that you will find him to be a true soul-companion.

CARL KOCH
Editor

✧ Introduction ✧

Is Praying with Francis for You?

Francis of Assisi is not for everyone. Even many saints would not be comfortable with Francis. He appeals primarily to the heart. He would never be accused of being lukewarm, for he lived his life afire. Francis found God in the concrete. He led a life of radical devotion to God and to service of other people, especially poor people.

Typically, Francis attracts the common folk more than the scholar. Devotions popular with many Roman Catholics are associated with Francis. The Christmas crib, stations of the cross, the stigmata, and garden statues surrounded by birds and flowers come immediately to mind.

Francis found his inspiration in the Gospels. More precisely, he found it in the stories in which Jesus walks among the people of the streets and talks with equal ease to children, tax collectors, lepers, foreigners, and Pharisees. Francis experienced the Good News enfleshed in poor people and in needy people, in fig trees and in mustard seeds, in sheep and in goats. In short, Francis practiced an incarnational, sacramental spirituality.

To say that Francis' vision is sacramental means simply that he was always drawn to the concrete, to the preciousness of things. He shunned intellectualizing and instead looked for God in the flesh, in the earth, in simple things. He preferred to pray with his feet, with his hands, and with his voice raised in song. Not only did Francis meditate on the suffering of Jesus, but he bore the wounds of Jesus in his very flesh when he received the stigmata.

The sacraments embody Christ's spirit, to which Francis was wedded. The sacraments speak of God through bread broken and shared, through cups of wine elevated and drunk, through water poured over and splashed upon a newborn baby, through oil that penetrates and leaves its mark on whatever it touches, through hands outstretched in blessing and welcome, and through rings, candles, and a change of clothes. Holy pictures, burning incense, ashes and palms, rosary beads, statues, the crowning of Mary with mayflowers—objects and practices known as *sacramentals*—would also please Francis.

For Francis, the stuff of the earth spoke of God's love. People and books and churches and crickets and earthworms were signs of love and revelations of God that should be taken to heart. Such devotion to the concrete does not appeal to everyone. Some people might even claim that it smacks of paganism or, at best, folk religion. However, Franciscan spirituality is clearly sacramental. It fits naturally into Christian tradition, and it resonates with the language and the stories of Jesus that we find in the Gospels.

Somewhere in our personality—that place in ourselves where we gleefully play and unself-consciously delight in the simplest of things—we can find a special corner in which to pray with Francis.

Francis in His World

The Flower of the Middle Ages

According to one story, when Pica Bernardone realized that she was about to give birth, a stranger suggested that she go to a nearby stable. The time was the late twelfth century. The setting was the northern Italian city of Assisi. In that stable, on straw surrounded by animals, Saint Francis was born. Overhead, angels heralded the event.

Thus, even Francis' birth is surrounded by legends. His life inspired many such stories. The legend of his birth in a stable illustrates how closely he mirrored Jesus. Already recognized as a great saint and a model of the Gospels during his life, Francis was officially canonized two years after his death.

Since Francis' time, many groups have claimed him for their own. His name is used by organizations dedicated to helping poor and outcast members of society. For instance, no more appropriate name can be found for a hospice for impoverished or homeless people than "Saint Francis Inn." Francis is a patron saint of charity as well as of social justice.

In the 1960s, Francis was heralded as the "hippie saint." For lovers of nature, he represents a kindred spirit. Advocates of peace look to him for inspiration. Those who warn against the dangers of materialism point to Francis as a shining example of living simply. Voices for equality in church and society point to his design for regulating the life of his companions—the "Little Brothers"—as a model of generous, simple, and purposeful living that continues to be relevant.

Francis' name has become associated with the Peace Prayer, one of the most popular prayers in Christian tradition. He suffered much, but he is renowned for advocating joy, song, and merriment. Today, followers of the way of this holy man of Assisi can be found in monastic solitude, in active religious communities, and in the lay calling.

We have very few writings by Francis. After all, he preferred action to words. We know the broad scope of his life and some of its details, but mostly we have brief stories *about* him. These anecdotes, called "little flowers," portray various dimensions of this multifaceted saint. Many of the little flowers are more legend than hard fact. When we read his life story, we find much that is appealing and encounter some episodes that might rankle, but throughout it we find an appealing and challenging person.

Francis took the commands of the Gospel literally. He was without compromise in his demands on himself and, although tempered with uncanny sensitivity, equally demanding of his followers.

From Riches to Rags

Francis lived during an era when power still resided with the nobility. However, a rising middle class was accumulating wealth and with it a desire for power, prestige, pleasure, pomp, and any other extravagances that money could provide.

Francis was born into this middle class. His father, Pietro, was a wealthy cloth merchant who could afford to provide his son with luxuries. In fact, Pietro was so enamored of style, romance, and "the good life" that he nicknamed his son (who had been baptized John) "Francis" after France, the country that he felt symbolized those qualities.

In his youth, Francis enjoyed the lifestyle that his father's money allowed. With his many friends from the town of Assisi, he engaged in boisterous, fun-loving pranks. He led his companions in singing, dancing, and merrymaking. Being cultured, good-humored, and companionable, Francis was evidently well-liked by the townspeople.

However, beginning with one of his youthful adventures, Francis' life underwent a radical change. Assisi went to war with its neighboring independent city-state, Perugia. Able to afford a horse and the paraphernalia of a knight, Francis joined the young men of Assisi in the feud. Francis' part in the action lasted only a short time. He was captured early in the battle and landed in prison. There he was treated deferentially because of his father's wealth and social position. According to legend, Francis' humor and good nature cheered his fellow prisoners.

A Change of Heart and Habit

Francis was soon released from prison, perhaps due to an illness that he contracted. When he returned home, he was a changed person even though he continued to revel with his old friends for a time. He frequently found himself lost in thought, meditating on his life. When he set out on another military campaign, he exchanged armor with a poorly clad knight along the way to battle and returned to Assisi without engaging the enemy. To his friends, Francis' constant state of distraction meant that he was in love. To Francis, it meant the same thing. However, the object of his love was not the lady whom his friends imagined, but "Lady Poverty."

From this point on, Francis set upon a journey that steadily led him away from the values and lifestyle of his society

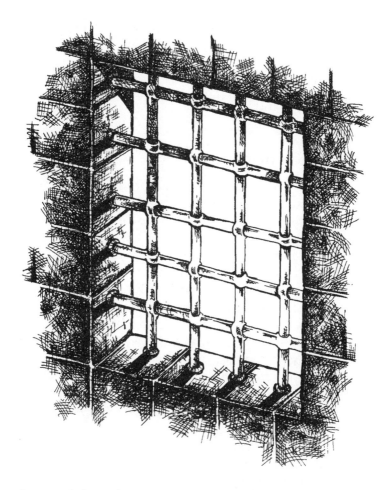

and toward the values and lifestyle of the Gospels. He recognized the glittering emptiness of his gilded age. He realized that by pursuing wealth and glory he was serving not the Master but false gods. He found gold coins and fine clothes to be lusterless compared to the beauty of Lady Poverty, through whom the greater beauty of sunsets and hillsides and of animals and fellow human beings of every social caste was revealed. He discovered not the fleeting pleasure of a night spent in revelry but the perfect joy that comes with intimately sharing in the passion of Jesus and in the suffering of other people.

His riches to rags story turns the Horatio Alger myth topsy-turvy. It gives flesh to the gospel message and still confronts us today.

The Treasure of the Gospels

Francis pursued his newfound treasure, the word of God, with such enthusiasm that most people who encountered him thought initially that he was mad. However, even with his radical turnabout Francis lost none of his earlier humor, joie de vivre, and charisma. If anything, these appealing qualities were enhanced by his transformation.

Obviously, Francis was onto something, although he himself was not quite sure what that "something" was. He knew that the gospel message contradicted much of what he saw in his society. In one gospel story, a rich young man is told to give his money to poor people. Francis took this to heart. In his early attempts to live the Gospel, he gave money to poor people more easily than he had spent it on his boon companions before his conversion. Since the money he gave away was actually his father's, Francis' generosity led to a famous confrontation during which he stripped himself naked, renounced his father's possessions, and declared himself a son of God. (At his death he expressed regret for rejecting his father.)

Assured by Jesus that the Holy Spirit would guide the actions of those who listened to God's word, Francis responded literally to a message he received while meditating before a crucifix in a small, run-down church: "Francis, do you not see that my house is falling down? Repair it!" He begged for stones and restored the little church.

In the stories in the Gospels, Jesus told his disciples to clothe the naked and to care for the sick. Francis overcame revulsion and kissed a victim of leprosy. For Francis, a loving caress to a despised and outcast person was a natural way to return love to the all-loving God.

A Light in the Darkness

Francis' actions ran counter to the spirit of his age. Nonetheless, he gained many followers who not only restored ruined churches but—through their dedication to gospel simplicity—breathed new life into a Church grown rich and complacent. Francis and his followers lived among the people, not apart from them as was the custom among earlier religious orders. Francis' brothers depended upon the generosity of others, as all beggars do. When the friars traveled to preach, they ate what was given to them and slept wherever shelter was offered. Sometimes they helped with planting or harvesting or did other temporary work to earn their bread. In this way—in the midst of city, town, and countryside—they served as an ever-present reminder of true Christian values, the only source of real joy.

Francis feared structure and definitive rules for his band of Little Brothers. His was a movement, a community of friends and companions, not an "Order" with a "Rule." The sole Rule for the friars was the Gospels. However, as his movement grew, pressures external and internal to the brotherhood combined to force Francis into composing a rule that adopted some of the structures of traditional religious orders.

Francis could never compromise his requirement of wholehearted acceptance—by his brothers—of the poverty spoken of in the Gospels. When church authority was brought to bear on him, he acquiesced to a less stringent rule, but afterward gradually divorced himself from the workings of the order that he had inspired.

Although the ideals of Francis were not always achieved by his followers even during his lifetime, his spirit has been one of the most potent and active forces within Christianity. Mention of a "Franciscan spirit" conjures images of simple, peace-filled, and joyful living that is in harmony with God and nature. This Franciscan spirit has come to be strongly identified with unique concern for and care of poor people.

Francis' Spirituality

Stories of Francis' life do not suggest a developed plan of action as much as they picture wholehearted commitment to God. His writing was minimal. He never sat down, pen in hand, to write a treatise on spirituality. But, in the course of his living, the following characteristics of Franciscan spirituality became clear: radical poverty; kinship with all people; oneness with nature; embrace of the enemy; appreciation for suffering, for peacemaking, for joy, and for companionship.

Radical Poverty

Francis came to despise money as something that separates people from one another. He recognized that money can entice us away from valuing people, animals, and things for what they are—creations of God. For these reasons, Francis counseled his followers to avoid touching money and to treat coins as they would pebbles that they found on the ground.

A Kinship with All People

Francis' belief in kinship among equally valuable human beings is revealed in the name he chose for his followers: Little Brothers. Francis declared that their only privilege was in having no privilege. Jesus shared in the lot of humanity; he was the Word made flesh, yet he claimed no privileges. If Jesus rejected the privileges of God, how much more should the Little Brothers live in kinship with all people.

Privilege implies power and powerlessness, haves and have-nots, nobility and commoners. Francis rejected any hierarchy among his followers. He desired that his Little Brothers have no Father Superior such as was common in religious orders of the time. To Francis, God alone was Father, and all others were brothers and sisters.

As with all elements of his spirituality, Francis practiced his beliefs. He never became a priest, and he cautioned his followers against reliance on the learned brothers to direct their group. While Francis was still relatively young and capable, he transferred leadership to another friar.

Oneness with Nature

Francis believed that all of God's creatures should be cherished, protected, and nurtured. His appreciation for the inherent value in all things found expression in anecdotes about Francis such as, "He would pick up any earthworms he found in his path and carry them to safety so that passersby would not tread them underfoot." In the "Canticle of the Sun," one of Francis' few writings, he referred to objects in nature as "brother" and "sister."

Embrace of the Enemy

Jesus told his followers to love their enemies. Francis' spirituality demonstrated his desire to love his enemies in many ways but perhaps most clearly in his attitude toward and treatment of Muslims. In the popular view of the time, Muslims were wicked profaners of the Holy Places and were enemies of Christ. They were labeled with all the derogatory epithets normally attributed to "the enemy" and were treated as such. To Francis, they were brothers and sisters who shared the same creator.

Francis directed some of his Little Brothers to live in Muslim lands—but not to fight them nor even to attempt to convert them initially. Rather, Francis instructed them to simply live the Christian virtues and in that way be a positive influence in Muslim society. Only after establishing the beauty and efficacy of these humble virtues should preaching take place. In this sense, the function of the Little Brothers was the same in Muslim countries as in Christian territory. Such equanimity toward members of another religion was considered radical in Francis' day and is uncommon even now.

Acceptance of Suffering

Francis came to embrace pain and suffering with the same gusto with which he embraced all dimensions of life. He found personal suffering to be a vehicle by which he could enter into the sufferings of others, especially the suffering of Jesus. An intense, mystical experience of the sufferings of Jesus resulted in his being marked with the stigmata—that is, with the imprints of the wounds suffered by Jesus on the cross. Francis encouraged the friars to look after their physical health but not to make a fetish of it. While he lay dying, he expressed his regret that he had not treated his body—"Brother Ass"—more kindly.

Peacemaking

Francis clearly recognized the ruinous link that connected accumulation of goods and prestige to violence and injustice. He knew firsthand the horrors of warfare. He saw town fighting town and factions fighting each other over claims to power and possessions.

Francis had great concern for the Crusades, the wars that were occurring between Christians and Muslims at the time. During the Fifth Crusade, he visited the sight of the fighting and found the plundering and unholy purpose of the Christian soldiers disgusting.

In contrast to the violence and aggression of the crusaders, Francis and a companion openly walked through enemy-held territory up to the tent of Sultan al-Kamil. He explained the true teachings of Jesus to the sultan, who listened with great interest and receptivity. The humble, peace-seeking Francis achieved a breakthrough of honest communication with Islam when the only achievements of the crusaders had been the chaos and noise of battle and the eerie silence of death.

Francis believed that by staunchly refusing to allow his followers to call anything their own, he was attacking the root cause of violence. When his local bishop suggested that his followers should provide for their own needs rather than depend on begging, Francis responded, "If we had possessions, we should need arms for their defense." As with all his teachings, Francis held himself accountable to this one to an extreme degree and used a radical example to underscore its importance. One time a brother told Francis, "I looked for you in your cell." Upon hearing the room in which he had been residing referred to as "your cell," Francis refused to stay there any longer.

Francis and his followers confessed that God is sole owner of the earth and all its goods. They believed that sharing goods—especially with poor and needy people—represents a necessary prerequisite to peacemaking.

Joy and Companionship

Francis and his early companions radiated joy—a childlike joy, a joy that frequently erupted into song, a joy described as a fire burning around about them.

The joy of Francis was the joy of the Beatitudes. It was the joy of the little ones, the lowly and the suffering, the persecuted ones. It was the joy of those who Jesus claimed would inherit the earth and constitute God's Kingdom. It was the joy of passionate involvement, an earthy, sensual joy. It was a joy intimate with suffering and yet joyful nonetheless. Francis experienced much personal suffering, felt deep compassion for the suffering of others, and still exuded joy even to the moment of his death.

Given his involvement with people, Francis was no solitary saint. In his youth, he passed his time in the constant company of friends. As his movement gained members, Francis wandered along the byways and throughout the towns with a troop of companions. Even when he sought solitude for private prayer, he would only remove himself from the ear-shot of his brothers. *Companion* literally means "sharing bread" with one another; Francis and his friends were true companions—they completely shared their bread and also received spiritual nourishment from each other in their times together.

Praying with Saint Francis

In following the Gospels, Francis strove to be uncompromising. We might be inclined either to dismiss him as a fanatic too extreme to be taken seriously or to place him on a pedestal, a saint whom we could never hope to imitate. However, even though Francis' contemporaries recognized him as an exceptionally saintly person, he remained engagingly human throughout his life.

Francis gave himself to worldly pursuits and found them wanting. He encountered Jesus and the Gospels in the humble creatures in his midst and discovered in them a source of true joy. He faced numerous struggles during his relatively short life, but he never wavered from his belief that the Gospels are a guidebook for living a full and wise life, a divine influence that leads people into passionate involvement in the world, and a treasure chest that contains the words of present and eternal joy.

While you are reading the stories about Francis, engaging in the reflections, and praying the scriptural passage for each meditation, imagine that your "Little Brother" from Assisi is present with you. He smiles the smile of one who sees himself as the lowliest of God's creatures but who, in spite of it, feels completely enveloped by God's love. He says to you, "Know God's love for you and live the Gospels. Above all, may Jesus give you peace."

✧ **Meditation 1** ✧

The Central Place
of the Gospels

Theme: Francis once instructed his friars, "We will learn through the gospels how the Lord instructed his disciples. . . . My brothers, this is our life and our Rule."

Opening prayer: I pray for a deep love of the Gospels and for the wisdom and courage to make them my agenda for action.

About Francis

After a time people began to be attracted to the humble way of life that Francis had chosen to lead, and two men came to him saying that they wanted to become his companions. Tomorrow morning we will go to church, he told them, and there we will learn through the gospels how the Lord instructed his disciples. In their simplicity they were unable to find the verses in the Holy Gospel which deal with renouncing the world, so they devoutly prayed that God would show them his will by the first words they should see on opening the book. Francis knelt before the altar with the Bible, and when he opened it he found the passage: If thou wilt be perfect, go and sell that thou hast and give to the poor, and thou shalt have treasure in heaven. He opened the Bible a second and a third time and read: Take nothing for your journey; and, if any man will come after me, let him deny himself. Francis thanked the Lord for having thus confirmed the resolution he already held in his heart, and he said to his two companions: My Brothers, this is our life and our Rule, and shall be so for all who wish to join our community. Go then, and act according to what you have heard! (Stephen Clissold, ed., *The Wisdom of St. Francis and His Companions,* pp. 30–31)

Pause: Reflect on this story.

Francis' Words

The Gospel was the Rule for Francis and his companions. He wanted to follow it exactly, but he knew that the Holy Spirit is constantly teaching us the meaning of the Gospels. Francis is recorded as telling his companions the following:

The Apostle says: *The letter kills, but the spirit gives life* (2 Corinthians 3:6). Those are killed by the letter who merely wish to know the words alone, so that they may be esteemed as wiser than others and be able to acquire great riches to give to [their] relatives and friends. In a similar way, those religious are killed by the letter who do not wish to follow the spirit of Sacred Scripture, but only wish to know [what] the words [are] and [how to] interpret them to others. And those are given life by the spirit of Sacred Scripture who do not refer to themselves any text which they know or seek to know, but, by word and example, return everything to the most high Lord God to Whom every good belongs. (*Francis and Clare,* p. 30)

Reflection

Francis insisted that the Gospels were the way to God and the guidepost for how to live life. Often he took the Scriptures quite literally. As his little band of companions grew in numbers and received approval from the pope, he desired that the Gospels remain the only Rule for his followers.

However, Francis understood the Gospels in the way that the first Christians knew them. During the first century of the Church, Christians did not have copies of the Gospels that they could carry around with them, but they did have the lived experience of the Spirit of Jesus as they encountered it in other believers and in their own deep-felt recollection of the bearer of the Good News. Together they shared their lived experiences (usually of suffering, persecution, and rejection), the stories of Jesus (his sayings and actions), and their special times together, such as during the breaking of the bread and the sharing of the cup.

Francis wanted to see in himself and in his companions the Gospels made flesh and therefore made credible to unbelievers and to those believers who held the Gospels at a distance. Francis and his companions sought to live the Gospels in spirit and in deed.

✧ Recall the passages or stories from the Gospels that have had the most influence on your life. Select one of the stories and meditate on all the ways in which this story has given you direction.

✧ Reflect on one person in the Gospels with whom you feel a close affinity. Why is this person so vital to you? What is God telling you through this person? Read some of the stories about this person again.

✧ As you read the newspaper, watch the news on television, or read about events of the world in magazines, who are the "saints" that live the Gospels and bring hope to the world?

✧ Whenever you put the word of God into practice, you are telling the story of Jesus once again. On paper or in your mind, compose one story from your life over the last few days that is the Good News. How have you been the Good News to the people around you?

God's Word

And as you go, proclaim that the kingdom of Heaven is close at hand. Cure the sick, raise the dead, cleanse those suffering from virulent skin-diseases, drive out devils. You received without charge, give without charge. Provide yourselves with no gold or silver, not even with coppers for your purses, with no haversack for the journey or spare tunic or footwear or a staff, for the labourer deserves his keep. . . .

Be prepared for people to hand you over to sanhedrins and scourge you in their synagogues. You will be brought before governors and kings for my sake, as evidence to them and to the gentiles. But when you are handed over, do not worry about how to speak or what to say; what you are to say will be given to you when the time comes, because it is not you who will be speaking; the Spirit of your Father will be speaking in you. (Matthew 10:7–20)

Closing prayer: O God, help me to hear the good news of your Gospel and to be the Gospel to those I meet. Amen.

✧   **Meditation 2**   ✧

Holy Poverty

Theme: "When a poor person approaches," Francis admonished, "always remember that the person comes in the name of Christ, who assumed our poverty."

Opening prayer: As poor persons, we stand in utter and absolute need, unable to go it alone. As poor persons, we stand dependent before our God, who knows our need and hears our cry. As poor persons we come to know the God who loves us as we are. As poor persons, we identify with all other poor persons. I pray that God will meet the needs of poor persons as I work to lighten their burdens and to share the earth's goods with them.

About Francis

While Saint Francis was preaching in a certain town, a poor man approached him begging for alms. Saint Francis felt very sorry for the man and commented on his sickly frame and general shabbiness. His companion answered, "Brother, it is true that he looks poor, but it could be a ruse; he could be the richest man in the province."

Saint Francis was enraged to hear this callous remark and said, "Take off your tunic and prostrate nude before that poor man, confess your words, and ask for forgiveness! When you sin against that poor man, you sin against

Christ. When a poor man approaches, always remember that he comes in the name of Christ, who assumed our poverty." (Lawrence Cunningham, ed., *Brother Francis*, pp. 128–129)

Pause: Reflect on your own attitudes toward poor persons.

Francis' Words

An old and poor woman who had two sons as friars once came to Saint Mary of the Angels to beg alms from Saint Francis. The saint went immediately to Brother Peter of Catania (who was the minister general at the time) and asked if there was anything to give the woman, adding that a mother of a friar was a mother of all friars. Brother Peter answered, "the only thing in the house is a copy of the New Testament, which we use to read the lessons during the night office." Saint Francis said to him, "Give her the Bible; it will be more pleasing to God that she should have it than we should read from it." Thus, she got the first New Testament that the brotherhood owned. (Cunningham, *Brother Francis*, p. 129)

Reflection

Poverty hardly seems like an ideal, given the millions and millions of people who live in squalor and abject poverty throughout the globe. Yet the heart of Franciscan spirituality is summed up in this one word—poverty.

For Francis, poverty is not living simply. He understood it and lived it literally. To live Franciscan poverty means to live without sufficiency, to be deprived and in a state of need and dependence. To be poor means precisely that—to be poor. In modern terms it means to be insecure and vulnerable, not knowing from one day to the next how the bills will be paid, where the next meal is coming from, where to get a job, or who might help us find decent housing. As in Francis' day, to be poor today means to be lumped into that nameless number known disparagingly as "the poor."

Is there any virtue in poverty? Not necessarily. Francis did not romanticize it. People who are poor can be as greedy and ruthless as anyone else. Poverty is virtue only in so far as it leads us to recognize that God alone can fill us and supply our every desire.

✧ In the excerpt in the section 'About Francis," Francis tells his companions, "When a poor man approaches, always remember that he comes in the name of Christ, who assumed our poverty."

Recall an instance when you encountered a poor person or a group of poor persons. How did you respond to them? Do you view rich people or middle-class people any differently than you view poor people? Should we view each group differently?

✧ Often we think that we should "give to the poor." In the spirit of Jesus and Francis, think about ways that you could receive from poor people and learn from them as well. If you are not poor, consider becoming involved in some activity that would result in your spending time with poor persons.

For further reflection, read the story of the widow's mite in Luke 21:1–4. Jesus remarks that the rich "put in money they could spare," while the widow "put in all she had to live on."

✧ Have there been moments in your life when you felt poor? Meditate on this statement of Jesus: "How blessed are you who are poor: the kingdom of God is yours" (Luke 6:20). In what way is Jesus speaking this to you?

✧ For several days, use the following statement by Jesus as a prayer during moments of inactivity: ". . . Wherever your treasure is, that is where your heart will be too" (Luke 12:34).

God's Word

And now a man came to him and asked, "Master, what good deed must I do to possess eternal life?" Jesus said to him, "Why do you ask me about what is good? There is one alone who is good. But if you wish to enter into life, keep the commandments." He said, "Which ones?" Jesus replied, "These: You shall not kill. You shall not commit adultery. You shall not steal. You shall not give false witness. Honour your father and your mother. You shall love your neighbour as yourself." The young man said to him, "I have kept all these. What more do I need to do?" Jesus said, "If you wish to be perfect, go and sell your possessions and give the money to the poor, and you will have treasure in heaven; then come, follow me." But when the young man heard these words he went away sad, for he was a man of great wealth.

Then Jesus said to his disciples, "In truth I tell you, it is hard for someone rich to enter the kingdom of Heaven. Yes, I tell you again, it is easier for a camel to pass through the eye of a needle than for someone rich to enter the kingdom of Heaven." When the disciples heard this they were astonished. "Who can be saved, then?" they said. Jesus gazed at them. "By human resources," he told them, "this is impossible; for God everything is possible." (Matthew 19:16–26)

Closing prayer: Help us, most loving God, to treasure the poor people in our midst, to share our goods, and to receive the gifts that poor people offer to us. Help us to not be angry or resentful toward them. Help us to know that we are, indeed, one of them before you. Amen.

✧ **Meditation 3** ✧

The Good Sense of Foolishness

Theme: Francis understood the good sense of foolishness, declaring, "The Lord said to me that he desired me to be a new sort of simpleton."

Opening prayer: I pray that I might join Francis in becoming a holy fool. I pray with Francis for the awareness that nothing is without its wonder and for the passion to give myself to life with humble and profound faith.

About Francis

A cardinal tried to persuade Francis to choose for the use of his companions one of the Rules followed by the Orders which already existed in the Church. God has called me by the way of simplicity and humility, Francis answered, and this is the way he wants me and my companions to follow. So I do not wish you to mention to me any other Rule—either that of St. Benedict, nor St. Augustine, nor St. Bernard, nor any way of life other than this way which has been shown and given me by God's mercy. The Lord said to me that he desired me to be a new sort of simpleton in this world, and that he would lead me by no other way than by that wisdom. (Clissold, *The Wisdom of St. Francis*, p. 72)

Pause: Ask yourself, how does being a simpleton have its own wisdom?

Francis' Words

Wishing to test the suitability of two young men who wanted to join his Order, Francis asked them to come with him into the garden, saying: Come with me and plant cabbages for the friars' food, just as you see me do. So he took the plants and put them in the earth upside down, with the roots above and the leaves under the ground. One of the young men, who was truly obedient, kept exactly to this way of planting, but the other, with a smattering of human wisdom, disapproved of this method as being unusual with gardeners, and declared that cabbages should be planted the other way round. Then Francis said to him: Son, imitate me, and do just as I do. But the other refused, thinking that what they were doing was foolish. Then the man of God said: Brother, I see that you are a great master. Go your way. For a simple and humble Order does not need such masters, but rather simple and foolish persons, like this companion of yours. (Clissold, *The Wisdom of St. Francis*, pp. 70–71)

Reflection

Wherever we turn these days we are surrounded by people giving us advice on how to live a balanced life, how to be "okay," or how to be assertive and to gain self-esteem. Whether we watch TV talk shows or tune in radio gurus, the advice is there for the listening. However, very few leaders invite us to live with a spirit of madness, a spirit of being on fire. Rarely are we encouraged to be passionate. As a result, Francis' call to zealous celebration and divine foolishness is deliciously enticing.

In the Scriptures, God is found in the fire of the burning bush of Moses, in the festive dance of Miriam after crossing the Red Sea, and in the sacred intoxication of a naked David dancing before the ark of the covenant. So enraptured were the Apostles after Pentecost that their hearers thought that they were drunk.

In the lives of the saints we encounter this divine madness and fire. These are not balanced lives where everything is okay. Look at Francis, or at Joan of Arc, who donned heavy armor in response to the voices she heard, or at the Roman priest Philip Neri, who as a confessor gave an overly scrupulous man the penance of walking through Rome wearing a live chicken in his hat. Modern examples abound too. Look at a Franz Jagerstatter, a Dorothy Day, a Gandhi, a Martin Luther King, Jr., or at a host of other "mad" people who are so "foolish" as to believe that our world can be transformed into a human community.

Of course the greatest fool, to those who had no heart to understand, was Jesus. The hard-nosed realists of his time plotted against him because of his outrageous behavior:

✦ He healed on the Sabbath—"Blasphemy!"
✦ He said that he would tear down the Temple and build it again in three days—"Madness!"
✦ He ate with sinners and tax collectors—"Impurity!"

The final madness was that Jesus gave eternal life through an ignominious death on the cross and subsequent resurrection. Jesus and Francis were fools and madmen to anyone who did not know that, as Emily Dickinson said,

> Much Madness is divinest Sense—
> To a discerning Eye—
> Much Sense—the starkest Madness.
> (*The Complete Poems of Emily Dickinson*, p. 209)

✧ A fine line often exists between foolishness and wisdom. Saint Paul says that faith in Jesus is foolishness to the Greeks. Make your own list of Jesus' teachings that appear to be foolish but are the profoundest wisdom, in other words, madness that is

> . . . divinest Sense—
> To a discerning Eye—

✧ Francis felt called to be a "new sort of simpleton." Do you feel the same call for yourself in any way? If so, how is it manifest in your life?

✧ Do you know some men or women whom you consider divinely foolish or Francis-like simpletons? Do you like them, or do you find them frightening and terrible? Would you invite them to dinner at your house?

✧ In the middle ages, Jesus was sometimes portrayed as a clown or jester. Recently, the musical *Godspell* has carried on this tradition. Do you feel that such a portrayal is appropriate?

God's Word

At this time the disciples came to Jesus and said, "Who is the greatest in the kingdom of Heaven?" So he called a little child to him whom he set among them. Then he said, "In truth I tell you, unless you change and become like little children you will never enter the kingdom of Heaven. And so, the one who makes himself as little as this little child is the greatest in the kingdom of Heaven." (Matthew 18:1–4)

At that time Jesus exclaimed, "I bless you, Father, Lord of heaven and of earth, for hiding these things from the learned and the clever and revealing them to little children. Yes, Father, for that is what it pleased you to do." (Matthew 11:25–26)

Closing prayer: O God of those who are foolish in the world's eyes, help me to know your wisdom hidden in the little ones in our midst and in the simple innocence within everyone's heart. Grant me divine madness. Amen. Alleluia!

✧　**Meditation 4**　✧

Blessed Peace

Theme: Francis taught his companions to use the greeting, "The Lord give you peace!" Peacemaking is almost synonymous with Franciscan spirituality.

Opening prayer: I pray for blessed peace. With Francis, I pray for the virtue to feel peace, to think peace, to speak peace, and to do peace—to be truly an instrument of God's peace.

About Francis

One day the Bishop of Assisi said to St. Francis: Your way of life without possessions of any kind seems to me very harsh and difficult. My Lord, Francis answered, If we had possessions we should need arms for their defence. They are the source of quarrels and lawsuits, and are usually a great obstacle to the love of God and one's neighbour. That is why we have no desire for temporal goods. (Clissold, *The Wisdom of St. Francis,* p. 32)

Pause: Reflect on the relationship between property and peacemaking.

Francis' Words

St. Francis taught his companions to use the greeting:
The Lord give you peace! When you proclaim peace by
your words, he told them, you must carry an even
greater peace in your hearts. Let no one be provoked to
anger by you, or be scandalized, but let your gentleness
encourage all men to peace, good will and mutual love.
For our calling is to heal the wounded, to tend the
maimed and to bring home those who have lost their
way. For many who today seem to us children of the
Devil will yet become disciples of Christ. (Clissold, *The
Wisdom of St. Francis*, pp. 31–32)

Reflection

Francis knew the power of words. He directed his companions
to greet one another with the words, "May the Lord give you
peace." He realized that quite often our words become real-
ities. For example, if we speak peaceably, we begin to feel
peaceful. From this inner peace comes the courage and convic-
tion to make God's reign of peace present again in our words,
in our work, in our very body. As a consequence, an environ-
ment of gentleness and peace is created.

Francis also knew the irony that peace involves struggle.
For instance, we struggle with our desire for revenge, greed,
and anger, wanting immediate satisfaction. In addition, peacemaking may require risking jail or death.

Early Franciscan history reveals the success of Francis' call
to peace. The original Third Order—laypersons who followed
Francis—abandoned their swords and other weapons. As a
result of this bold step, peace came to the Italian city-states.

✧ Reflect about your use of language. Recalling conver-
sations that you have had over the last two days, did you use
any harsh or violent words? Are these a regular part of your
vocabulary?

Now recall words of consolation, joy, or peace that you
shared with other people.

✧ Make today's newspaper part of your prayer for peace. Flip through the pages, reading the headlines. When you come to a story about violence, spend a few moments praying for peace and reflecting about how you might help bring peace to this situation. When you come to a headline that shows people making peace, offer your praise and thanks to God.

✧ Is there anyone with whom you need to make peace? Imagine the faces of people with whom you might need reconciliation. Ask Jesus' help to make peace, and then try to design a realistic plan for making peace with this person. Reconciling with one's enemies is a richly fruitful prayer.

✧ For Francis, poverty, simplicity, humility, courteousness, and all the other virtues that he advocated led to peace. What virtues do you possess that serve as fertile ground for peace?

God's Word

You have heard how it was said to our ancestors, You shall not kill; and if anyone does kill he must answer for it before the court. But I say this to you, anyone who is angry with a brother will answer for it before the court; anyone who calls a brother "Fool" will answer for it before the Sanhedrin; and anyone who calls him "Traitor" will answer for it in hell fire. So then, if you are bringing your offering to the altar and there remember that your brother has something against you, leave your offering there before the altar, go and be reconciled with your brother first, and then come back and present your offering. . . .

You have heard it said: Eye for eye and tooth for tooth. But I say this to you: offer no resistance to the wicked. On the contrary, if anyone hits you on the right cheek, offer him the other as well; if someone wishes to go to law with you to get your tunic, let him have your cloak as well. And if anyone requires you to go one mile, go two miles with him. Give to anyone who asks you, and if anyone wants to borrow, do not turn away.

You have heard how it was said, You will love your neighbour and hate your enemy. But I say this to you, love your enemies and pray for those who persecute you; so that you may be children of your Father in heaven, for he causes his sun to rise on the bad as well as the good, and sends down rain to fall on the upright and the wicked alike. For if you love those who love you, what reward will you get? Do not even the tax collectors do as much? And if you save your greetings for your brothers, are you doing anything exceptional? Do not even the gentiles do as much? You must therefore set no bounds to your love, just as your heavenly Father sets none to his. (Matthew 5:21– 48)

Closing prayer: God of peace, may I become an instrument of your peace, in my thoughts, in my words, and in my actions. I ask this through Jesus, the Prince of Peace. Amen.

✧   **Meditation 5**   ✧

Courtesy

Theme: When Francis looked at others, "he only saw the image of God multiplied but never monotonous" (G. K. Chesterton, *St. Francis of Assisi,* p. 96). And to all people, Francis showed holy courtesy.

Opening prayer: I pray for holy courtesy—for the virtue of treating others as I would like to be treated. I pray for an all-inclusive respect for other creatures that is the seedbed of a human and global community.

About Francis

Brother Ruffino contemplated and prayed so much that he was very withdrawn, rarely spoke, and became almost a recluse. Nor did he have much ability in preaching or the use of words. Nonetheless, one day Saint Francis told him to go to Assisi and preach to the people using the words that God would inspire him to use.

Brother Ruffino, on hearing the order, said to Saint Francis, "Reverend father, I beg you not to send me, for, as you know, I have no talent for preaching, being an unlettered, simple, and not too bright soul." Saint Francis answered, "Because you did not obey with alacrity, I order you to strip down to your breeches, walk through the city of Assisi, find a church there, and preach to the people."

At this order Brother Ruffino stripped himself and naked made his way to Assisi. Entering a church, he genuflected before the altar, climbed up into the pulpit, and began to speak. Children and men alike began to laugh and cry out, "Look at him! They have done so much penance, they have gone crazy."

Saint Francis, in the meantime, began to think about the obedience of Brother Ruffino, a man who was one of the most noble of Assisi. It was a harsh order to give, and he began to reprove himself: "What presumption you have, son of Pietro Bernardone, you wretched little creature. How dare you send Brother Ruffino, one of the noblest men of Assisi, to walk through the streets naked like some madman. By God, you will do the same thing that you have ordered the other to do."

With that, he stripped naked and departed right off for Assisi, taking with him Brother Leo (who was clothed), who carried his habit and that of Brother Ruffino. As he came near the town, the citizens began to taunt him, thinking that he had gone crazy from his excessive penances.

Saint Francis went into the church where Brother Ruffino was preaching in these words: "My beloved people, flee the world; avoid sin; help each other if you wish to avoid hellfire; observe the commandments of God; love God and your neighbor if you wish to go to heaven; do penance if you wish to possess the heavenly kingdom." Saint Francis, completely nude, then ascended the pulpit and began to preach so powerfully . . . that the people, on hearing it, all began to cry with copious tears. A vast number of men and women felt great devotion and compunction of heart.

Soon what happened in the church overflowed into the whole city, so that the passion of Christ had never been mourned more than on that day. The people were edified and consoled by Saint Francis and Brother Ruffino. Saint Francis dressed Brother Ruffino, and the two of them headed back to Saint Mary of the Angels, praising and glorifying God, who had given them the grace to forget and humiliate themselves for the edification of the flock of Christ, who learned about despising the world. They acquired such a reputation of holiness from this incident that the people thought it was a grace just to touch the hem of their garment. (Cunningham, *Brother Francis,* pp. 73–75)

Pause: Reflect on the place of holy courtesy in your life.

Francis' Words

Francis ended his "Prayer Inspired by the Our Father" in this way:

> and may we love our neighbors as ourselves
>> by drawing them all with our whole strength to Your love
>> by rejoicing in the good fortunes of others as well as our own
>> and by sympathizing with the misfortunes of others
>> and by giving offense to no one
>>> (*Francis and Clare,* p. 105)

"The Earlier Rule" of the Friars Minor includes this directive:

> . . . And whoever comes to [the brothers], friend or foe, thief or robber, should be received with kindness. And wherever the brothers are and in whatever place they meet other brothers, they must greet one another wholeheartedly and lovingly, and honor one another without complaining *(1 Pet 4:9). (Francis and Clare,* p. 115)

Reflection

G. K. Chesterton had this to say about Francis and courtesy:

> I have said that St. Francis deliberately did not see the
> wood for the trees. It is even more true that he deliberate-
> ly did not see the mob for the men. What distinguishes
> this very genuine democrat from any mere demagogue is
> that he never either deceived or was deceived by the illu-
> sion of mass-suggestion. Whatever his taste in monsters,
> he never saw before him a many-headed beast. He only
> saw the image of God multiplied but never monotonous.
> To him a man was always a man and did not disappear in
> a dense crowd any more than in a desert. He honoured all
> men; that is, he not only loved but respected them all.
> What gave him his extraordinary personal power was
> this; that from the Pope to the beggar, from the sultan of
> Syria in his pavilion to the ragged robbers crawling out of
> the wood, there was never a man who looked into those
> brown burning eyes without being certain that Francis
> Bernardone was really interested in *him;* in his own inner
> individual life from the cradle to the grave; that he him-
> self was being valued and taken seriously, and not merely
> added to the spoils of some social policy or the names in
> some clerical document. Now for this particular moral
> and religious idea there is no external expression except
> courtesy. (*St. Francis of Assisi,* pp. 96–97)

Francis believed that we are all relatives. We owe care,
compassion, and mannerliness to all creatures, whether they
are members of the human family or of our extended family in
the nonhuman realm. The courtesy of Francis is not simply a
medieval quaintness but a profound recognition of God's presence in everything.

For instance, Francis would have understood and valued
the custom of the Taos Indians who walk barefoot on the
grounds of their pueblos for a prescribed period of time. These
Native Americans feel that the earth must be reverenced and
respected, and this annual ritual serves as a living reminder of
that. Because God is present in everything, no one is superior.
Everyone and everything is special. Everyone and every creation deserves courtesy.

✧ What are some courtesies that you extend to people so naturally that you almost forget that you do them? Recall your acts of courtesy for the last two days (remember that courtesy is treating others as you wish to be treated). How do you feel about these courtesies? How could you build even more courtesy into your life? List as many ways as you can think of. Then offer these acts to Jesus.

✧ If the weather permits, spend some time walking barefoot on the earth. As you walk, praise the creator for Sister Earth and resolve to treat her courteously.

✧ Imagine that you are looking into the mirror in the morning before you leave for your day's work. What mental comments do you make to yourself? Try to list some of these. Are your comments mostly negative? Would you feel better if you glanced in the mirror every morning and said, "I am a valuable, lovable person, created in God's image"? Should you not be courteous to yourself too? Offer this prayer each morning.

✧ How conscious are you of your own status and that of other people? Does being conscious of status ever influence your behavior? Spend some time reviewing the last couple of weeks. How does being conscious of status relate to courtesy?

✧ Think of persons or groups to whom you have difficulty showing respect or being courteous. Imagine that Jesus encounters them. How would he react to them?

God's Word

Do not judge, and you will not be judged; because the judgments you give are the judgments you will get, and the standard you use will be the standard used for you. Why do you observe the splinter in your brother's eye and never notice the great log in your own? And how dare you say to your brother, "Let me take that splinter out of your eye," when, look, there is a great log in your own? Hypocrite! Take the log out of your own eye first, and then you will see clearly enough to take the splinter out of your brother's eye. . . .

So always treat others as you would like them to treat you; that is the Law and the prophets. (Matthew 7:1–12)

Closing prayer: O God, you are creator and lover of all that is, and through your son, Jesus, you remind us that your divine spark burns within us and our world. I pray that I may share in your vision. By seeing your image in all creatures, may I and all my fellow creatures more clearly image you. Amen.

✧ **Meditation 6** ✧

Right Action

Theme: Francis sought to serve God in all matters. To do so required action, not just words.

Opening prayer: God, send me holy courage to respond to people in pain, to take action in time of crisis, to restore the Church where it is crumbling, to affect a world in need, to be a living, breathing, active instrument of God's peace.

About Francis

Francis wanted his followers to be in the marketplace, in the streets, and in the towns. Indeed, he wanted his followers to be in the thick of things, building bridges to God. This story, "Sultan Malik-al-Kamil," shows Francis to be a person of fearless action.

> As on the day in a robber-infested forest [when] he had proclaimed himself the Herald of the Great King, Francis went forward singing. He sang the psalm that David sang while his sheep grazed in peace beside still waters. He addressed God with the same faith that the lamb puts in his shepherd: "The Lord is my shepherd, I shall not want."
>
> The river along which the two brothers walked was not still. The waters, swollen by the rains, roared along swiftly and spread out into an immense troubled expanse stretching to the horizon of the desert. Not a house was to

be seen, not a plant, a cultivated field, a living person—everything had been burnt, sacked, destroyed, in the furious haste of the retreat.

But above the noise of the swirling river rose Francis's strong voice, filling the forbidding emptiness: "Yea, though I walk through the shadow of the Valley of Death, I shall fear no evil, for thou art with me."

They found two sheep browsing tranquilly and believed them to be a sign sent by divine providence. Francis . . . rejoiced over them and said to his companion, "Place all your trust in God, because the words of the Gospel will be fulfilled in us, 'Remember, I am sending you out to be like sheep among wolves.'"

The wolves fell upon them a little farther along. Warriors of the sultan's army attacked them, seized them, shouted incomprehensible threats, and beat them so savagely that the two travellers believed that they had been called to receive the palm of martyrdom they so much desired. Amid all this, they incessantly called out the name of the sultan, and the Saracens finally decided that they must be ambassadors with propositions from the leaders of Christians who wished to abjure their faith. So they tied them up securely and led them to Kamil.

And this is how it happened . . . that the leading exponents of the two religions and the two civilizations, so long and so incessantly at war with each other, found themselves face to face. (Arnaldo Fortini, *Francis of Assisi*, pp. 427– 429)

Pause: Reflect on Francis' fearless action.

Francis' Words

Francis was once told that at Paris the brothers had chosen as their Master a learned Professor of Theology who greatly edified both clergy and laity. I am afraid, he said with a sigh, that such men will end by killing my little plant. The true Masters are those who set an example to their neighbours in good works and kindness. For a man is learned in so far as he works for others; he is wise in so far as he loves God and his neighbours; and he is a good preacher in so far as he knows how to do good works faithfully and humbly. (Clissold, *The Wisdom of St. Francis*, p. 53)

Reflection

That Francis had little time for books or discussions is hardly a secret. Unceasingly and without hesitation he put into action the words of Jesus. He was not a quaint little "saint" fit only for a birdbath, nor a flower child, nor an innocent, as he is sometimes portrayed. Rather, he was a practical dreamer on pilgrimage to an awesome God.

His message and his methods mirror those of Jesus. Over the centuries, many Christians have tried to divorce spirituality from human action. Viewing as religious only those attitudes or practices specifically found in the Scriptures or in a church is tempting. In the spirit of Francis, God is acting all around us, for God acts in human beings who are willing to heal, to bridge the gaps, and to struggle on behalf of poor and suffering people. The love of God is poured out through the actions of God's children.

✧ Jesus told us to love God and to love our neighbors as ourselves. Try to list all the times that you have loved other people in the last three days; especially note the ways that you have fostered the good of others by acting on their behalf.

✧ Each moment presents opportunities for acts of charity. Consider several acts of kindness that you have wanted to put into action but have not for one reason or another. Plan to act for someone in need. Carry out the act as part of your prayer.

✧ Many times, small acts of love and concern are over-looked. Love often comes to us in small gifts. Recall several specific expressions of concern that were extended to you in the last twenty-four hours. Thank God for each act of kindness.

✧ Our workplace is an area in which we are called to act as Jesus did. Imagine that you are talking to Jesus about your work. Dialog with Jesus about how you can be an example of hope, faith, and love in your job. Some people find that writing the dialog can be helpful; you write your comment to Jesus, and then Jesus responds. Talk to Jesus about how you can be a "little brother or sister" in your work.

✧ Find one passage from either 'About Francis" or "Francis' Words" that most touches you. Meditatively read the passage several times, perhaps emphasizing a different word each time. Then ask God to explain what meanings the passage has for your life.

✧ Select one short passage from any of the readings in this meditation: for example, "Make me an instrument of your peace," or "I shall fear no evil, for thou art with me." Use this passage as a prayer that you can say several times during your day to remind yourself that God's love for humankind is shown through your actions.

✧ What group or organization do you now belong to or would you like to join that works for the values of Jesus?

God's Word

It is not anyone who says to me, "Lord, Lord," who will enter the kingdom of Heaven, but the person who does the will of my Father in heaven. . . .

Therefore, everyone who listens to these words of mine and acts on them will be like a sensible man who built his house on a rock. Rain came down, floods rose, gales blew and hurled themselves against that house, and it did not fall: it was founded on rock. But everyone who listens to these words of mine and does not act on them will be like a stupid man who built his house on sand. Rain came down, floods rose, gales blew and struck that house, and it fell; and what a fall it had! (Matthew 7:21–27)

Closing prayer: Conclude your meditation with the Peace Prayer, making the words truly your own.

Loving God, make me an instrument of your peace.
Where there is hatred, let me sow love;
Where there is injury, pardon;
Where there is doubt, faith;
Where there is despair, hope;
Where there is darkness, light;
And where there is sadness, joy.
O, Divine Teacher, grant that I may not so much seek to
    be consoled as to console;
To be understood as to understand;
To be loved as to love;
For it is in giving that we receive;
It is in pardoning that we are pardoned;
And it is in dying that we are born to eternal life.

✧ Meditation 7 ✧

Simplicity

Theme: "Having nothing, yet possessing all things" is a paradox that springs from the Gospels and is a constant motif in Francis' life.

Opening prayer: I pray for holy simplicity, so that I may enjoy the simple things—time with family and friends, the beauty of nature, the joy of realizing God's love for humankind.

About Francis

A cardinal, seeing what virtuous lives the friars led, thought it would be of benefit to the Church if some of them were made bishops. But Francis answered him: We have been called Friars Minor and may not presume to become of more account. If you wish us to bear fruit in God's Church, keep us rather in this state to which we have been called, and even force us back to lowliness against our will. (Clissold, *The Wisdom of St. Francis*, p. 73)

Pause: Reflect on Francis' response to the cardinal.

Francis' Words

Francis feared that learning would make his friars proud and they would then lose their humility and love of poverty. Just suppose, he said, you had subtlety and learning enough to know all things, that you were familiar with all languages, the course of the stars, and everything else—what is there in that to be proud of? A single demon knows more on those subjects than all the men in this world put together. But there is one thing that the demon can never learn, and which is the chief glory: to be faithful to God. (Clissold, *The Wisdom of St. Francis*, p. 78)

Reflection

Simplicity is not poverty. Simplicity means that we live close enough to the limits of our resources that we can rely on God's love for us and appreciate the unadorned wonders of Creation. The gift of simplicity is found in the man or the woman who can be thankful for humble beauty. If we take time to look at the marvels of the world, we cannot help but lift our heart to God in thanksgiving. The goal of Franciscan simplicity, and what today is called "simple living," is to encourage us to live in joy!

Simplicity supports the celebration of life. Francis advocated simplicity and realized that simplicity and the enjoyment of life's goods are linked. As with all elements of Franciscan spirituality, his commitment to simplicity mirrors Jesus' example. Jesus appreciated wine, food, health, loving, birds, caring touch, children, women, men, storytelling, and other good things of the earth.

Simple living is not always simple to do. Considerable thought is required to sort out what is necessary, what is luxury, and what is just plain silly. We are pressured not to be satisfied with having just enough, not to be generous and warmhearted, and not to enjoy the goodness of people. Instead we are pressured to acquire more possessions. Francis challenges us to enjoy life, not to own it.

✧ A driving force of modern society is consumerism, the drive to possess things to such a degree that we become possessed ourselves. Name ways that consumerism has affected your life. Has it led to true joy, false happiness, or added hardship for you?

✧ Reflect on the statement "Simplify your life!" How would you do it? Try to outline a "simplicity of life" plan. What would you give away? What would you keep? What are all the ways that you could enjoy life without spending money?

✧ The Franciscan spirit of simple living can be applied to our relationships with God and other people. For example, do you frequently rely on material gifts to show affection? Name one way that you could practice simplicity toward others and toward God.

✧ A prayer that you might use frequently to remind yourself of the goodness of simple living is from a Shaker hymn:

'Tis a gift to be simple;
'Tis a gift to be free.

God's Word

Do not store up treasures for yourselves on earth, where moth and woodworm destroy them and thieves can break in and steal. But store up treasures for yourselves in heaven, where neither moth nor woodworm destroys them and thieves cannot break in and steal. For wherever your treasure is, there will your heart be, too. . . .

No one can be the slave of two masters: he will either hate the first and love the second, or be attached to the first and despise the second. You cannot be the slave both of God and of money.

That is why I am telling you not to worry about your life and what you are to eat, nor about your body and what you are to wear. Surely life is more than food, and the body more than clothing! (Matthew 6:19–25)

Closing prayer: Thank you, God, for the simple things and the true treasures in my life, such as [mention some treasures in your life]. For these and for all your good gifts, I thank you, God. ". . . Give me neither poverty nor riches, grant me only my share of food, for fear that, surrounded by plenty, I should fall away and say, 'Yahweh—who is Yahweh?' or else, in destitution, take to stealing and profane the name of my God" (Proverbs 30:8–9). Amen.

✧ **Meditation 8** ✧

Serving Our Neighbors

Theme: The statement "For it is in giving that we receive," from the Peace Prayer, could serve as a summary of Francis' way of life.

Opening prayer: In the spirit of Francis, I pray for the gift of seeing God in persons in need and for the courage to serve them in joy.

About Francis

One day [Francis] was riding on horseback down the road to the hospital, as usual absorbed in his thoughts. Suddenly the horse jerked to the side of the road. With difficulty Francis pulled him back by a violent jerk at the reins. The young man looked up and recoiled in horror. A leper stood in the middle of the road, a short distance away, . . . the usual wan specter, with stained face, shaved head, dressed in grey sackcloth. He did not speak and showed no sign of moving, of getting out of the way. He looked at the horseman fixedly, strangely, with an acute and penetrating gaze.

An instant that seemed eternity passed. Slowly Francis dismounted, went to the man, took his hand. It was a poor emaciated hand, bloodstained, twisted, inert and cold like that of a corpse. He put a mite of charity in it,

pressed it, carried it to his lips. And suddenly, as he kissed
the lacerated flesh of the creature who was the most abject, the most hated, the most scorned, of all human beings, he was flooded with a wave of emotion, one that
shut out everything around him, one that he would remember even on his death bed.

As the leper withdrew his hand, Francis raised his
head to look at him again. He was no longer there. . . .

Francis remounted and continued on his way. But the
whole world seemed changed, and he, too. He saw that
the mysterious words that had come to him earlier had
now become a revelation of truth. He had opened his
heart to what he had in the past held in horror, and the
bitterness of it had become changed into sweetness of the
same measure.

After several days he took some money and went to
the hospital near Arce. He crossed the threshold that had
filled him with horror, went along the dark corridors,
knocked at cell doors on which the cross was nailed. The
lepers gathered in a frightening assembly in the chapter
hall. They waited, astonished and suspicious. To each of
them Francis gave a piece of gold and a kiss on the lips.
(Fortini, *Francis of Assisi*, pp. 211–212)

Pause: Imagine Francis kissing the leper.

Francis' Words

In the course of the thirteenth century, the people granted
many privileges to this hospital, the Assisi hospital of San
Lazzaro. The bull in which they were granted began:
"The lepers' hospital, which stands on the site where the
Order of St. Francis had its beginning . . ." Such a statement is, even by the most rigid historical definition, exact.
In that hospital a basic rule of a harder chivalry was laid
down, one that required passion and valour over and beyond the measure needed by armour-covered warriors
leading in attack.

That rule is *compassion*. For all the sorrowing, the
troubled, the ill, the victims of disaster and those over-

come by shame, misery, weariness, and oppression. Those kept down because of blindness or folly, subtle evil or hatred, lust for money or pleasures of the flesh.

To cleanse human beings from whatever leprosy contaminates them was the mission on which Francis embarked the day that he went to see the diseased patients of the hospital of San Lazzaro.

Before dying he dictated a few brief, impassioned words, part of his *Testament* to establish the exact turning point for him. "This is how God inspired me, Brother Francis, to embark upon a life of penance. When I was in sin, the sight of lepers nauseated me beyond measure; but then God himself led me into their company, and I had pity on them. When I had once become acquainted with them, what had previously nauseated me became a source of spiritual and physical consolation for me." (Fortini, *Francis of Assisi*, p. 212)

Reflection

After his experience with the leper, Francis recognized that following Jesus meant serving humankind. Stories abound of how he and his community lived out Jesus' example of washing the feet of his disciples. Francis first worked with lepers, the most neglected and despised group in his society.

He preached in the streets, trying to empower poor and underprivileged people with hope and courage. He traveled to the Crusades, trying to establish peace. He invited the civic authorities of neighboring cities to be reconciled with one another. He saved animals from destruction.

The paradoxical power of Francis' message lies in its being *mutual ministry:* by serving others, he was converted. Francis calls the Church to feed the hungry, to be with the AIDS patient, to stand by the single parent, to organize for decent neighborhoods, to meet pressing needs in cities or wherever poor people are gathered. By serving these people, the servant can be converted.

Franciscan prayer is always oriented to the marketplace, hospital, jail, neighborhood, hospice, to families at odds with each other, to the business world, the community of nations, the churches, and members of world religions. It is the prayer of ordinary people. This prayer is practical and tough, for it is found in people willing to meet the living God—as Francis met God in the leper by the side of the road—in the suffering and ugliness of daily life. Franciscan prayer is prayer-in-action.

✧ Meditate on these words of Francis: "When I had once become acquainted with them, what had previously nauseated me became a source of spiritual and physical consolation for me." How can these words teach you compassionate service?

✧ Most of us are afraid of some disease or condition that inflicts our brothers and sisters. Take a personal inventory of diseases or conditions that most strongly repel you. What is it that repels you? How would you react if a person with one of these diseases or conditions met you on a lonely path and asked for your assistance? Try to imagine such a scene and your response. Then put yourself in the other person's shoes; imagine his or her reaction to you. Finish this reflection by asking yourself what service lepers—people who repel us—do for us.

✧ One of the most important aspects of Franciscan spirituality is praying the experiences of the day. That is, we reflect on who we are this day as God sees us. Each day is a chance to serve our neighbors, maybe through friendliness, maybe by doing our work competently, maybe by volunteering in a soup kitchen, maybe by being an AIDS caregiver. Pray the experiences of the last twenty-four hours. Talk to God about how you served your brothers and sisters and how they served you. Every experience is a message from God, teaching us how to be more Jesus-like.

✧ Francis viewed involvement in service not as contradictory to pursuit of joy but as the source of true joy. Does this express truth for you? Recall a time when service to other people was a rich experience of joy for you.

✧ While serving poor people in El Salvador, Jean Donovan and three religious women were killed by a death squad. Shortly before she died, Jean Donovan said: "You can . . . make a big difference in the world if you realize that the world you're talking about might be very small—maybe one person, or two people. . . . If you can find a place to serve, you can be happy" (Ana Carigan, *Salvador Witness*, p. 96). Francis would agree. Think of instances when you have made a big difference in the world—even if that world consisted of only one or two persons. How can you continue to serve and to make a big difference?

God's Word

When the Son of man comes in his glory, escorted by all the angels, then he will take his seat on his throne of glory. All nations will be assembled before him and he will separate people one from another as the shepherd separates sheep from goats. He will place the sheep on his right hand and the goats on his left. Then the King will say to those on his right hand, "Come, you whom my Father has blessed, take as your heritage the kingdom prepared for you since the foundation of the world. For I was hungry and you gave me food, I was thirsty and you gave me drink, I was a stranger and you made me welcome, lacking clothes and you clothed me, sick and you visited me, in prison and you came to see me." Then the upright will say to him in reply, "Lord, when did we see you hungry and feed you, or thirsty and give you drink? When did we see you a stranger and make you welcome, lacking clothes and clothe you? When did we find you sick or in prison and go to see you?" And the King will answer, "In truth I tell you, in so far as you did this to one of the least of these brothers of mine, you did it to me." (Matthew 25:31–40)

Closing prayer: I pray we, the Church, will be known for service, so that—like Francis—we will be converted to Christ, who is manifest in those people in need in our midst. Amen.

Littleness

Theme: To emphasize the virtues of simplicity and humility, Francis decided that his followers should be called "the Order of the Little Brothers."

Opening prayer: In the spirit of Francis, I pray for a spirit of littleness, so that I may experience the joy of being what I am—a child of God.

About Francis

One day blessed Francis said, "The Order and life of the Friars Minor is a little flock which the Son of God has asked of His heavenly Father in these latter days, saying, "Father, I would that Thou shouldest form and give Me a new and humble people in these latter days, who will be unlike all who have preceded them in humility and poverty, and content to possess Me alone." And the Father said to His beloved Son, "My Son, it is done as Thou hast asked."

So blessed Francis used to say that God willed and revealed to him that they should be called Friars Minor, because they were to be the poor and humble people whom the Son of God had asked of His Father. Of this people the Son of God Himself speaks in the Gospel: "Do not be afraid, My little flock. Your Father has determined to give you His kingdom." And again: "Believe Me, when you did it to one of the least of My brethren here, you did it to Me." And although the Lord was speaking of all poor and spiritual people, He was referring more particularly to the Order of Friars Minor which was to arise in His Church. (Fortini, *Francis of Assisi*, pp. 314–315)

Pause: Reflect on the word *little.*

Francis' Words

On one occasion Francis admonished the members of his community with these words:

Let no one appropriate to himself the role of being over others.
I did not come to be served but to serve (cf. Mt 10:28), says the Lord. Those who are placed over others should glory in such an office only as much as they would were they assigned the task of washing the feet of the brothers. And the more they are upset about their office being taken from them than they would be over the loss of the office of [washing] feet, so much the more do they store up treasure to the peril of their souls (cf. Jn 12:6). (*Francis and Clare*, p. 28)

Reflection

An essential component of Francis' spirituality (one could say "the heart of the matter") is his sense of being a child of God. Remember his words spoken in the plaza before the bishop and townspeople on the day that he disowned his father, Pietro Bernardone: "I no longer call you father for I have only one Father in heaven." At this turning point in his life, Francis intensely realized that he was a child of God.

As a child of God, Francis could throw himself into God's arms in utter dependence on and complete surrender to God's direction. As a child, he could celebrate the wonders of creation. He could rejoice in the freedom of belonging to a gracious God who is mother and father. Francis experienced that he was loved and treasured by this loving presence.

Therefore, Francis protected his followers from honors and status that would keep them from knowing the joy of being children of God. He named them the Little Brothers, or Friars Minor. Francis accepted into his band those who were considered ordinary, even simple. Any of his followers who were from the nobility or educated elite had to live as Little Brothers too.

Similarly, the child inside each of us—a little brother or sister—can bask in the glory of the sensuous world and experience the sacramental delight of God's gifts. The child inside knows the pleasure of being alive. Freed from a need for manipulation and control, the little one inside each of us simply appreciates and gives thanks.

Francis challenges us to let our little child out into the sunlight. He challenges us to unchain ourselves from the need to control, to rationalize, or to think that we can take all the world's problems on our shoulders. He knew that we stand in relation to God as babies stand in relation to their mothers and fathers: completely dependent, thoroughly in awe, and crying to be nourished.

✧ Find pictures of yourself as a baby and as a young child. If you have a scrapbook of your childhood, slowly page through it, recollecting memories of the events celebrated in the pictures. The past is filled with painful moments certainly, but concentrate for now on the times of wonder, joy, and love, the times of simpler, more innocent, treasured experiences.

As you page through the photos a second time, reflect on these questions: "Do I still appreciate and relish the little pleasures? Is the child in me still alive, still wondering, and still happy about the simple beauty around me?"

✧ Imagine that you are with Jesus in the Garden of Olives. Night has fallen. Jesus sits exhausted on the ground, leaning back on one of the gnarled olive trees. You do likewise.

You imagine what he must be feeling, knowing that he is about to be betrayed unto death, his disciples leaving him to face his agony alone. His face is twisted in pain and sorrow. Jesus looks up into the heavens and, sighing, raises his hands up to God, saying, 'Abba, not my will but yours be done."

Having said these words, Jesus' face becomes suffused with calmness. He turns toward you and asks, "My friend, lift up to Abba all the things that cause you anxiety and disappointment."

You want to tell Jesus all your worries, like children unburden themselves to loving parents. And so you tell Jesus all that you fear.

When you have poured out your grief, Jesus says, "God loves you. Say with me, 'Abba, not my will but yours be done.'"

You repeat Jesus' offering, 'Abba, not my will but yours be done." You repeat this prayer over and over.

✧ Think of the children you encounter each day. Do you enjoy their presence? What do they teach you about life?

✧ Francis is said to have initiated the custom of setting up crib scenes at Christmas. To hearts that are open, every day is a celebration of Jesus' coming. If you have a Christmas creche scene, find it and set it up. Meditate on the child Jesus, the Word made vulnerable, dependent, wondering flesh.

God's Word

"See that you never despise any of these little ones, for I tell you that their angels in heaven are continually in the presence of my Father in heaven."

"Tell me. Suppose a man has a hundred sheep and one of them strays; will he not leave the ninety-nine on the hillside and go in search of the stray? In truth I tell you, if he finds it, it gives him more joy than do the ninety-nine that did not stray at all. Similarly, it is never the will of your Father in heaven that one of these little ones should be lost." (Matthew 18:10–14)

Closing prayer: Like Brother Francis, I know that I am your child, my loving God. I know that you "have engraved [me] on the palms of [your] hands" (Isaiah 49:16) and that you will never forget me. Amen. Alleluia!

✧ Meditation 10 ✧

Glorious Nature

Theme: Francis proclaimed, "We are sister and brother to animals and plants, water and soil, earth and sky." Just as we meet the dancer in her dance, the painter in his art, and the poet in her finely crafted words, so we encounter the creator in Creation. Indeed, we are nature aware of itself, consciously creating itself, celebrating itself and its creator.

Opening prayer: I pray *with* God's good Creation, of which I am a part, remembering that to spend time with my sisters and brothers in nature is praying—being with God.

I pray *for* God's good Creation. Like all creatures, we humans play a special role in Creation—not to be above nature or apart from nature but to *care for* nature.

About Francis

Once when Francis was passing near a certain village he noticed a large flock of birds of different kinds all gathered together. Leaving his companions and going eagerly towards them, as they seemed to be awaiting him, he gave them his accustomed greeting. Surprised that they did not fly away as they generally do, he started talking to them: Brother birds, you ought to praise and love your Creator very much! He has given you feathers for clothing, wings for flying, and everything you need. He has made you the noblest of his creatures, for he has appointed the pure air for your habitation. You have neither to sow nor to reap, yet he takes care of you, watches over you and guides you. At this the birds began to rejoice after their fashion, stretching out their necks, spreading their wings, opening their beaks and looking at him, whilst he went to and fro amongst them, stroking their heads and bodies with the fringe of his tunic, and finally making the sign of the cross over them and sending them away with his blessing. (Clissold, *The Wisdom of St. Francis*, pp. 59–60)

Pause: Recall a favorite scene from nature.

Francis' Words

Praised be thou, my Lord, with all your creatures,
especially Sir Brother Sun,
Who is the day and through whom You give us light.
And he is beautiful and radiant with great splendor;
and bears a likeness of you, Most High One.
Praised be You, my Lord, through Sister Moon and
    the stars,
in heaven You formed them clear and precious and
    beautiful.
Praised be You, my Lord, through Brother Wind,
and through the air, cloudy and serene, and every kind
    of weather
through which You give sustenance to Your creatures.
Praised be You, my Lord, through Sister Water,
which is very useful and humble and precious and
    chaste.
Praised be You, my Lord, through Brother Fire,
through whom you light the night
and he is beautiful and playful and robust and strong.

Praised be you, my Lord, through our sister
    Mother Earth,
who sustains and governs us,
and who produces varied fruits with colored flowers
    and herbs.

. . . .

Praise and bless my Lord and give Him thanks
and serve Him with great humility.

(Francis and Clare, pp. 38–39)

Reflection

Francis and the birdbath are a common sight. We feel a sentimental tug when we think of this holy man and the birds. Like Jesus before him, Francis knew the power and joy of rejoicing in the blessings of God, that is, the blessings of nature.

Francis reminds us that nature includes not only animals but ourselves, our body and our soul. That is, nature is catholic; it includes all that is. Nothing is left out. Even the deserts and wastelands are included, and they are holy and beautiful. All is a blessing. Hence we rejoice in our God who is artist and lover, and with Francis we celebrate that in our home—the universe—we are all family.

Francis would understand the Native American boy of sixteen who tells about how he spent an afternoon off from school. "I went to my favorite place in the mountains. No one else knows this special place but me and one other friend. I sit in the silence for hours, and I listen to the trees or the sky or the animals speaking to me. This particular day I heard the trees."

This young man from Saint Catherine's Indian School in Santa Fe is studying to be a medicine man. For him, God's Spirit heals through nature; in his words, "We need to listen well if we want God's healing to touch us." Francis would agree.

✧ As part of this prayer, if possible, take a short journey out into the open. Go for a walk or bicycle ride, or just sit outside and bask in Creation. Be present to the wind, the sky, the sounds, and the smells. Perhaps you could respond to this litany of impressions with "Praise God!" For example, "For the swaying walnut trees, praise God!"

✧ Take some soil in your hand. Look at it; smell it. For a few moments, imagine all the ways in which we depend on the soil. Let these images come to mind and register and change, like flash cards. Then let the soil run out of your hand back to the ground, saying "Praised be thou, my Lord, for our sister Mother Earth." Repeat this prayer slowly, letting its meaning nourish you like the soil nourishes life.

✧ If you cannot go outside for a prayer-journey, you may wish to make a prayer-journey from your memory. Read these directions carefully, then close your eyes and make the journey.

Try to sit as comfortably as you can. Generally, it helps to have both feet resting on the floor; rest your arms in your lap—preferably uncrossed because crossing arms or legs cuts off circulation.

Relax. Close your eyes. . . . For a few moments, slowly breathe in . . . and out. . . . Focus on slow, relaxed breathing. . . . Now give your body a chance to relax too.

Now place yourself in a scene from nature, a favorite spot from a vacation, or compose in your imagination a comforting, beautiful scene with all of your favorite sights, animals, birds, flowers, and trees. . . . Just bask in the wonder of Creation.

As you are relaxing in nature, Jesus comes to you. . . . He says, "Peace be with you." . . . He sits next to you. . . . The two of you relax in each others presence and in the presence of Creation. . . .

✧ Compose your own canticle to your sisters and brothers in Creation. Pray it frequently, and add to it as you experience nature in new ways.

✧ As an examen of conscience, recall two ways in which you have cared for Mother Earth over the last two days. Then think of two ways in which you could show more respect for Mother Earth.

✧ When was the last time you set aside time to appreciate God's gift of a sunrise or sunset? How could you learn to love nature better? Francis treated all creatures as brothers and sisters, with gentleness and respect. Do your patterns of consumption reveal a gentle spirit toward other creatures, or do they show abuse of Creation?

✧ Skim through the Gospels. Take note of the nature imagery used by Jesus in his teaching. Choose one image to be the focus of your meditation for a day.

✧ Find a line from "Francis' Words" (see pages 71–72) that speaks most powerfully to you. Pray this line over and over. Use this line as a prayer throughout your day.

God's Word

Look at the birds in the sky. They do not sow or reap or gather into barns; yet your heavenly father feeds them. Are you not worth much more than they are? Can any of you, however much you worry, add one single cubit to your span of life? And why worry about clothing? Think

of the flowers growing in the fields; they never have to work or spin; yet I assure you that not even Solomon in all his royal robes was clothed like one of these. Now if that is how God clothes the wild flowers growing in the field which are there today and thrown into the furnace tomorrow, will he not much more look after you, you who have so little faith? So do not worry; do not say, "What are we to eat? What are we to drink? What are we to wear?" It is the gentiles who set their hearts on all these things. Your heavenly Father knows you need them all. Set your hearts on his kingdom first, and on God's saving justice, and all these other things will be given you as well. So do not worry about tomorrow: tomorrow will take care of itself. Each day has enough trouble of its own. (Matthew 6:26–34)

Closing prayer: Complete your meditation with a prayerful reading of these words from the Psalms.

> Praise God from the heavens;
> praise God in the heights; . . .
> praise God, sun and moon;
> praise God, all you shining stars. . . .
> Let them praise the name of God,
> who commanded and they were created. . . .
> Praise God all the earth, . . .
> fire and hail, snow and mist,
> storm winds that fulfill God's word.
> You mountains and all you hills,
> you fruit trees and all you cedars,
> you wild beasts and all tame animals,
> you creeping things and flying birds. . . .
> Be this God praised by all the faithful ones. . . .
> Alleluia.
>
> (Psalm 148)

✧ **Meditation 11** ✧

Humility

Theme: "I ask of God no privilege except that of having none." This comment by Francis explains his life of humility.

Opening prayer: I pray for holy humility, the ability to see and accept myself as I am—stuff of the earth and a temple of God's Spirit.

About Francis

One day, when Francis was coming out of a wood where he had been praying, Brother Masseo went to meet him. Wishing to put his humility to the test, he said to him, affecting a jeering tone, Why *you?* Why *you?*

What do you mean by that? Francis asked him.

I mean, why should it be *you* all the world is running after, and why does everybody want to see you, listen to you and obey you? You are not handsome, nor very learned, nor of noble birth. Why, then, should all the world be running after you?

When Francis heard this, he rejoiced in the spirit and raising his face to heaven, he remained a long time with his mind uplifted to God; after a while, returning to himself, he fell on his knees and gave praise and thanks to God. Then he turned to Brother Masseo in great fervour of spirit and said: You want to know why it should be me the world is running after? This is granted me because the eyes of the most high God, which look upon the good and the evil in every place, could not find among sinners anyone more vile, worthless and sinful than me, or any baser creature on earth for the marvellous work he intends to perform. So he has chosen me to confound the nobility, the greatness, the power, the beauty and the wisdom of the world. He has done this that men may understand that all virtue and all good proceed from him alone, and not from any creature. (Clissold, *The Wisdom of St. Francis*, pp. 49–50)

Pause: Reflect for a moment on the fact that all good comes from God alone.

Francis' Words

Francis showed great tenderness for all of God's creatures, however humble. Remembering the Psalmist's words: As for me, I am a worm and no man, he would pick up any earthworms he found in his path and carry them to safety, so that passersby would not tread them underfoot. (Clissold, *The Wisdom of St. Francis*, p. 47)

The friars once complained to Francis: Can you not see that the bishops often do not let us preach, and we are frequently made to wait for days on end before we are allowed to proclaim the word of God? It would be best to obtain from the Pope a privilege to allow us to preach. It would be for the good of souls. Francis answered them: I would rather see the prelates first converted by humility and respect. For when they have seen us humble and respectful towards them, they themselves will beg us to preach and convert the people. As for me, I ask of God no privilege except that of having none, and to be full of respect for all men, and to convert them, as our Rule ordains, more by example than by our words. (Clissold, *The Wisdom of St. Francis*, p. 63)

Reflection

Humility comes from the Latin words for "earth" and "on the ground." To be humble means that we know the truth not only of our earthly limitations but also of our divine giftedness. In humility, we have our feet planted "on the ground," knowing our real state, which is complete dependence on the will of our God, who nurtures, gifts, and loves us.

Rooted in the experience that God gives us everything that we need, we are freed from fear and self-absorption and empowered to nurture the needy, share our gifts, and love our neighbors as ourselves. In this way, humility is freeing and empowering. Francis lived this spirit of humility. He was boldly self-forgetful and equally respectful to pope and to earthworm.

✧ Humility requires a sense of humor. Praise God for the times in your life when you laughed at yourself—perhaps when you realized that you were taking yourself too seriously or when you succeeded at something in spite of yourself.

✧ Is there any situation in your life right now that you find humbling? How can this situation be God's call to continuing conversion? What attitude could you bring to this situation so that it could become freeing and empowering for you?

✧ Humility is a virtue that reminds us of the pain and glory of our human condition. Compose a litany of thanksgiving for all the reminders in your life that tell you that you are not God but a fallible, needful human being who is nurtured and protected by a loving God: for instance, "For my inability to stay on my diet, thank you, God." Then make a litany of thanksgiving for all the gifts of skills, talents, and personality that God has given you: for example, "For my sense of humor that others enjoy, thank you, God." You might write down your litanies so they can be reminders for you.

✧ Name examples of the humility of Jesus.

✧ The next time that you are at Communion, meditate on the following words: "By the mystery of this water and wine may we come to share in the divinity of Christ, who humbled himself to share in our humanity."

God's Word

Then the mother of Zebedee's sons came with her sons to make a request of him, and bowed low; and he said to her, "What is it you want?" She said to him, "Promise that these two sons of mine may sit one at your right hand and the other at your left in your kingdom." Jesus answered, "You do not know what you are asking. Can you drink the cup that I am going to drink?" They replied, "We can." He said to them, "Very well; you shall drink my cup, but as for seats at my right hand and my left, these are not mine to grant; they belong to those to whom they have been allotted by my Father."

When the other ten heard this they were indignant with the two brothers. But Jesus called them to him and said, "You know that among the gentiles the rulers lord it over them, and great men make their authority felt. Among you this is not to happen. No; anyone who wants to become great among you must be your servant, and anyone who wants to be first among you must be your slave, just as the Son of man came not to be served but to serve, and to give his life as ransom for many. (Matthew 20:20–28)

Closing prayer: Blessed are you, merciful God, for the gift of earth and of our own earthiness. Like a potter, you fashioned me from the clay of the earth, yet this earthly body of mine can rejoice in freedom and peel into laughter at the humor of my human condition. Accept the humble gift of who I am as you humbly gave yourself to us in your son, Jesus. Amen. Alleluia!

The Church

Theme: "Francis, rebuild my church." This message from God to Francis inspired him not only to rebuild the physical structures of the Church but also to seek its rebirth and reformation as a community.

Opening prayer: In the spirit of Francis, I pray for the Church so that we may be a Church in love with one another and carry on the work of Jesus as members of his body.

About Francis

The church of San Damiano seemed to be collapsing from old age, already beyond repair, desolate, without devout worshippers and without prayers. No one went down the worn staircase into the church. No lamp burned in front of its altar. Decrepit outer walls, cracked inner walls, crumbling bricks, worm-eaten beams, faded paintings. A low smoke blackened vault, a narrow window, a holy water stoup covered with dust, an apse with vague vestiges of blue and gold, a cloister invaded by wild grass, a well without water. Silent, solitary, abandoned. On the travertine architrave of the door, the usual words so often found on the thresholds of ancient country chapels: *Domus mea.* My house. The House of God, tottering and derelict.

The painted wooden image of the Crucified Lord that hung by the altar had survived all that decay—an image of goodness and suffering, expressing with extraordinary vividness both martyrdom and love.

One day, going up to the city, Francis went into the church, knelt, and began to pray. He asked to be given light in the midst of all his darkness, to know the divine will, in accordance with the promise made during the night in Spoleto.

Suddenly it seemed to him that Jesus' gaze was fixed on him. There was no doubt about it. Those eyes had become animated, taken on life. They were speaking and expressing a burning passion. And, as in the night of the vision of the enchanted castle, the cavalier consecrated to a high undertaking distinctly heard his name being called. The words fell like a whisper, a light sigh, scarcely perceptible.

"Francis, go and repair my house, which, as you see, is falling into ruin."

After a short pause, the sad call was repeated for the second time, for the third time.

Francis got up, frightened. The church was again sunk into a silence without beginning or end. He went out, sought the old priest who had custody of the place, and offered him all the money he had with him so that he might relight the lamp before the crucifix.

Then he rushed up to Assisi. He went to the shop and took down some scarlet, the noblest and most expensive cloth that then existed, used for making mantles suitable for the grandeur of kings and elaborate gowns with trains for beautiful women. Francis wanted to use it to cover the poor abandoned church in sumptuous purple. (Fortini, *Francis of Assisi*, pp. 215–216)

Pause: Hear God's call to Francis, "Repair my house."

Francis' Words

Saint Francis being already full of the grace of the Holy Spirit called the six brothers together in the wood surrounding Saint Mary of the Angels where they often gathered to pray; and there he foretold many future things.

"Dear Brothers, let us consider our vocation, and how God, in his great mercy, called us not only for our salvation but for that of many; and to this end we are to go through the world exhorting all men and women by our example as well as by our words to do penance for their sins, and to live keeping in mind the commandments of God." And he added: "Do not be afraid to preach penance even though we appear ignorant and of no account. Put your trust in God who overcame the world; hope steadfastly in him, who, by the Holy Spirit, speaks through you to exhort all to be converted to him and to observe his commandments. You will find some men to be faithful and kind and they will receive you gladly; but you will also find many who are unfaithful, proud and blasphemous, and they will insult and injure you and your words. Therefore prepare your hearts to suffer everything humbly and patiently." (P. 925)

They were constant in prayer and in working with their hands; this they did in order to banish idleness, the enemy of the soul. They rose at midnight and prayed with many sighs; and each deeply loved the other and cared for him as a mother cares for a cherished only child. Charity burned so ardently in their hearts that it was easy to risk life itself, not only for love of Jesus Christ, but also for the soul and body of any one of the brothers. (Marion A. Habig, ed., *St. Francis of Assisi*, pp. 929–930)

Reflection

The call of Francis at San Damiano is similar to the call of the Apostle Paul. In both cases, they were not "called" to individual salvation. Rather they were alerted to the mystery of Christ found in the community initiated by baptism, the Church. Francis was converted—"turned around"—to Jesus and discovered him in the faithful people who week after week gather for Eucharist and who clearly need one another. For Francis, the church building needed rebuilding, but so did the Church, the Body of Christ.

During the time of Francis, the Church had become like the society of which it was a part—rich, self-serving, and stuffy.

The compassionate face of Christ was obscured by the facade of bureaucracy and pomp. It desperately needed rebirth.

To many Christians of his day, the spirit of Francis was like water in the desert. The followers of Francis began to live the Gospel in small groups and with such warmth and sincerity that people around them were reminded once again of the early Christians when they realized that they were Christ's body. Like Christ, the early Christians healed the sick, fed the hungry, protected the poor, confronted evil, set free those bound, and even raised the dead to life. The followers of Francis resembled this early Church. They lived the Gospel in such a way that the people of Assisi could see the beauty of Jesus in their own time. Francis and his companions imitated Jesus and the first Christians by preaching the Good News to the poor.

For Francis, Jesus and his Church were one and the same. For him, the Church was family—the extended family of sisters and brothers throughout the globe sharing the Gospel of Christ.

✧ The Church can be seen from several different angles.

✦ *The Body of Christ:* the community of believers who are the physical expression of Jesus on earth.

✦ *An Institution:* a group of persons organized for a similar purpose.

✦ *A Sacrament:* a sign of God's saving love.

✦ *The Herald of God's Word:* the official messenger to proclaim the Word of God to all people everywhere.

✦ *The Servant:* in the name of Jesus, the servant of the human family, following the Beatitudes.

Reflect on ways that the Church effectively fills these five roles. As a part of the Church, how have you participated in each of these roles of the Church? Meditate on which of these roles is most meaningful for you and on which one causes you the most confusion.

✧ God told Francis to "repair my house." When you consider your experience in the Church, where does God's "house" most need repair now? How are you called to "repair my house?" What special talents could you contribute to the Church's rebirth?

✧ Over time, conflicts arise in any group of people. Even though the Church is called to be a loving community, things happen. We can become alienated from the Church or some aspects of it. Francis would wish us reconciled.

Recall one or two incidents by which you felt hurt by the Church or a person in the Church. Let your memory be specific as to people, place, events, time, and feelings.

When you have recalled the incident(s), read this guided meditation. When you know the outline of it, close your eyes, relax, and enter into the reflection:

Imagine Jesus present in the scene of your alienation. . . . He listens to you and to the other people. . . . The conflict is laid out before Jesus. . . . Finally, you ask him what he thinks. . . . Ask Jesus to bring you to understand the conflict and to lead you to some act that expresses your reconciliation. . . . Talk back and forth with him about this reconciliation. . . . Finally, Jesus says, "My friend, let go of your anger and go forth in peace.". . . Open your hands palm up and imagine the anger and alienation leaving your grasp. . . . Thank Jesus for being with you.

God's Word

. . . [Jesus said], "Who do you say I am?" Then Simon Peter spoke up and said, "You are the Christ, the Son of the living God." Jesus replied, "Simon, son of Jonah, you are a blessed man! Because it was no human agency that revealed this to you but my Father in heaven. So I now say to you: You are Peter and on this rock I will build my community. And the gates of the underworld can never overpower it. I will give you the keys of the kingdom of Heaven: whatever you bind on earth will be bound in heaven; whatever you loose on earth will be loosed in heaven." (Matthew 16:15–19)

There are many different gifts, but it is always the same Spirit; there are many different ways of serving, but it is always the same Lord. There are many different forms of activity, but in everybody it is the same God who is at work in them all. The particular manifestation of the Spirit granted to each one is to be used for the general good. To one is given from the Spirit the gift of utterance expressing wisdom; to another the gift of utterance expressing knowledge, in accordance with the same Spirit; to another, faith, from the same Spirit; and to another, the gifts of healing, through this one Spirit; to another, the working of miracles; to another prophecy; to another, the power of distinguishing spirits; to one, the gift of different tongues and to another, the interpretation of tongues. But at work in all these is one and the same Spirit, distributing them at will to each individual. (1 Corinthians 12:4–11)

Closing prayer: Jesus, help me to nourish your Body, to herald your word, to be a sign of your presence, to serve humankind as you would. Amen. Alleluia!

Struggle

Theme: "Holy Father, release me from my sins but not from the vow to follow our Lord Jesus Christ." This request of Saint Clare to the pope, who wished to lighten the demands of absolute poverty for the early Franciscan sisters, indicates the willingness to struggle that was so characteristic of Francis.

Opening prayer: In the spirit of Francis, I pray for patience, courage, and clarity of purpose during times of struggle.

About Francis

Clare [Francis' beloved friend] knew that she would be able to serve Francis in no better way than to remain faithful to his great principle, Poverty. Therefore, in contrast to other monasteries that asked the pope the concession of special privileges to safeguard their vast possessions, she asked Innocent III to grant them the privilege of possessing nothing. The pontiff observed that never had such a privilege been asked of the court of Rome.

With his own hand he wrote out the text of this Privilege of Poverty. . . .

'As is manifest, you, wishing to dedicate yourselves solely to God, have renounced every desire for temporal things; and to that end, having sold all your goods and distributed what was gained to the poor, you propose to have no possessions in any way, wanting to follow the footsteps in everything of the One who for us made himself poor, thus becoming the way, the truth, and the life. And you are not frightened by the lack of necessary things in this intention, so long as the right hand of your celestial Spouse is under your head to support the weakness of your body, which you have disciplined to be subordinate to the rule of your will. After all, he who feeds the birds of the air and clothes the lilies of the field will not fail you in both food and clothing, until such time as you gain eternal life, when he will minister to you himself, and his right hand will reach out to embrace you most joyfully in the fullness of his sight.

'And, therefore, as you have asked, we with apostolic favour approve your aim of highest poverty, granting, with the authority of this writing, that by no one may you be forced to receive possessions.". . .

Pope Gregory IX, who was so fond of Clare that he often visited her, suggested to her one day that she accept some goods that would allow her and her companions to live without anxiety for the future. To this, . . . Clare objected with a ferocity unimaginable in a creature so sweet and delicate.

. . . The memory of Francis must have turned Clare's heart upside down in that moment, for she, not without a quiver of contempt, replied to the head of the church, "Holy Father, release me from my sins but not from the vow to follow our Lord Jesus Christ." (Fortini, *Francis of Assisi*, pp. 360–361)

Pause: Reflect on Clare's strength of purpose.

Francis' Words

The father, Pietro Bernardone, spoke first. In his usual irate tone of voice, which not even the solemnity of the assembly caused him to soften . . . , he repeated his accusation, told of his indignation, asked punishment of the guilty. His son could no longer remain in the bosom of the family after having offended it so gravely, going about dressed in rags, thinking he could get off scot-free for all the outrageous things he had done. . . .

The bishop said, turning to Francis: "You have disturbed and shocked your father very much. Give him back his money and he will be placated. In other ways God will provide for the restoration of his church.". . .

"Lord Bishop," he said, "not only this money that I took from him do I wish to restore to him, with all good will, but even the clothes that he has given me."

The words were a sudden inspiration for Francis, knight of Christ. . . .

Every tie between Francis and his family was now cut. Now he was alone, with only his love. . . .

"Up until today I have called Pietro Bernardone my father. For the future I shall say, 'Our Father, who art in heaven. . . .'" (Fortini, *Francis of Assisi*, pp. 228–229)

Reflection

In trying to understand the dimension of struggle found in the prayer of Francis, we do well to look at Clare of Assisi, his first woman follower. Clare exemplifies the ideal Christian as envisioned by Francis.

Clare lived the cloistered life for over forty-two years. (She outlived Francis.) Clare was a woman of intense prayer. This intensity enabled her to stand firm and to defend her beliefs. After she left to join Francis and his followers, Clare had to struggle against her family, who at one point tried to bring her back home by using bodily force. From tradition, another image of Clare shows her with a monstrance in her hand, warding off invading Saracens. Not only did she successfully stop the Saracens, but she also resisted cardinals and popes who wished to soften the Franciscan ideal of poverty.

For Francis and Clare, prayer enabled believers to rely on God and, together with God's Spirit, to stand firm in the face of being tempted to compromise the Good News.

In the midst of struggle, patience is received through prayer. Patience does not mean empty, fruitless waiting. The word *patience* means "to suffer with." To stand in the face of opposition, misunderstanding, and hostility as Francis did (because of his commitment to Lady Poverty) required "suffering with" his adversaries and with his companions. To confront her family, Clare had to "suffer with" them. Communicating with their God in prayer strengthened the patience of Clare and Francis.

✧ Find one phrase in the two readings from *Francis of Assisi* that most touches you. Read the phrase slowly several times. What particular message is the Spirit directing to you?

✧ Remember a time when you had to stand up and be counted for what you believed. What was at issue? Who were your adversaries? How did you behave? What were your feelings? Did you seek God's support and wisdom?

✧ Bring to mind a struggle in which you are engaged now. What matters of principle are involved? How are your adversaries suffering too? Can you put yourself in their shoes? After all, patience is "suffering with."

In order to "suffer with" your adversaries in the struggle in which you are engaged now, put yourself in a three-way discussion about the matters at issue. To do this, put three chairs in a circle. Imagine that you are your adversary, Jesus, and yourself (you take all three parts). Begin this dialog by stating your side of the issue. Then take the part of your adversary. Next let Jesus speak. Continue this order of conversation until you have thoroughly talked out the issue.

End this meditation by making some kind of plan to resolve the issue with your adversary in a way that Jesus would approve. Pray for patience in the struggle.

✧ List the issues of peace and justice for which you would be willing to struggle. Assess how far you would be willing to commit yourself to these struggles. For example, for some issues you might pray, but for others you may be willing to demonstrate or even engage in nonviolent civil disobedience. Finally, for each issue answer this question: "How would Francis engage in the struggle about this issue?"

God's Word

"Do not suppose that I have come to bring peace to the earth: it is not peace I have come to bring, but a sword. For I have come to set son against father, daughter against mother, daughter-in-law against mother-in-law; a person's enemies will be the members of his own household.

"No one who prefers father or mother to me is worthy of me. No one who prefers son or daughter to me is worthy of me. Anyone who does not take his cross and follow in my footsteps is not worthy of me. Anyone who finds his life will lose it; anyone who loses his life for my sake will find it." (Matthew 10:34–39)

Closing prayer: Patient God, I pray not for an absence of struggles in my life, but for the patience and discernment needed to make the difficult decisions in the struggles that I face. Amen.

Worship

Theme: "Lift up your hearts to the Lord" was a frequent admonition of Francis to his companions. Worship was integral to Francis' relationship with God.

Opening prayer: In the spirit of Francis, with the heavens and the earth, I praise and thank you, God. I lift my heart to you.

About Francis

The saint of God was clothed with the vestments of the deacon, for he was a deacon, and he sang the holy Gospel in a sonorous voice. And his voice was a strong voice, a sweet voice, a clear voice, a sonorous voice, inviting all to the highest rewards. Then he preached to the people standing about, and he spoke charming words concerning the nativity of the poor King and the little town of Bethlehem. Frequently too, when he wished to call Christ *Jesus*, he would call him simply the *Child of Bethlehem*, aglow with overflowing love for him; and speaking the word *Bethlehem*, his voice was more like the bleating of a sheep. His mouth was filled more with sweet affection than with words.

Besides, when he spoke the name *Child of Bethlehem* or *Jesus*, his tongue licked his lips, as it were, relishing and savoring with pleased palate the sweetness of the words. The gifts of the Almighty were multiplied there, and a wonderful vision was seen by a certain virtuous man. For he saw a little child lying in the manger lifeless, and he saw the holy man of God go up to it and rouse the child as from a deep sleep. This vision was not unfitting, for the Child Jesus had been forgotten in the hearts of many; but, by the working of his grace, he was brought to life again through his servant St. Francis and stamped upon their fervent memory. At length the solemn night celebration was brought to a close, and each one returned to his home with holy joy. (Habig, *St. Francis of Assisi,* p. 301)

Pause: Picture Francis with the Child Jesus.

Francis' Words

Francis made friends with a cricket. It happened like this. In the Porziuncola woodlands one day, in the burning dog-days, a cricket breaks the empty noonday silence with its song. The brothers, who had risen before dawn to recite the hours, are asleep. So now in the merciless heat the praises to the Lord are sung by the cricket. Her song is almost too much as it pours out of the fullness of her joy. The parched fields, the thirsty streams, the dusty roads, resound with it.

Francis, motionless among the still oaks, listens, enraptured. He is overcome by the desire to take into his hand this wonderful sister, who can make her wings, a weft and woof of steel, become a ringing lyre. He is delighted by this little creature from which comes such vibrant harmony, who can sing alone or, although in solitude, join a chorus of other crickets. The cricket sings for herself, for the cloud passing over the hill, for the frond

stretching over the still water, for the blade of grass awaiting the morning breeze. But she falls silent when people
approach, suspecting the worst.

Even this distrust was overcome when Francis calls,
"My sister cricket, come to me."

And the cricket comes immediately from a hiding
place in a fig tree into his hand.

Francis says, "Sing, my sister cricket, and praise your
Creator with a joyful song."

And the cricket begins to sing again. She sings and
sings while Francis, enthralled, listens to her and praises
her. He speaks to her about his thoughts, his desires, his
dreams. He speaks of God who is splendour and harmony. He talks of light and shadow, of beautiful life and silent death.

Finally he lifts his hand and the cricket returns to its
tree. Eight days pass and the cricket does not move from
that tree. When Francis leaves his cell, she is ready to fly
to his hand, to sing or be silent according to his com-
mand. At the end of that time Francis says to his companions, "Let us give our sister cricket leave to go, for it has
made us sufficiently happy now. We do not want our
flesh to glory vainly over things of this kind."

So the cricket takes flight beyond the tree and is lost
in the sky. It never returns. (Fortini, *Francis of Assisi*, pp.
541–542)

Reflection

Francis may be remembered for the Christmas crib, the stations
of the cross, devotion to the passion of Jesus, and retreats in the
mountains. When we think of liturgical renewal within the
Church, probably very few of us call Francis to mind. More read-
ily we think of Benedict and the monasteries and movements
dedicated to liturgical prayer. However, to pray in the spirit of
Francis is indeed to be united with the Church at worship.

Francis prayed the Liturgy of the Hours. He prayed morning and evening prayer with his brothers. The Little Brothers

were always supposed to have a companion with whom to pray. His devoted friend Clare and her company of poor women spent their days in this same liturgical rhythm of the rising and setting sun. Francis' vision and life were supported, sustained, and challenged by Christ and his body, the Church, in its worship.

Within the Church's liturgical prayer, the moments of each daily cycle were filled with an awareness of God. The day, the week, and the year were lived with "hearts lifted to the Lord" in gratitude.

Francis kept the Sabbath. He loved the Lord's day. His followers throughout the ages have remained faithful to the Sabbath tradition of the Church: Eucharist, psalms for morning and evening, as well as the sacred tradition of rest, creativity, play, and delight. Work is put aside. All are invited to rejoice in the beauty of God's Creation. All are invited to the feast of heaven on earth.

✧ Read the story of Francis and the cricket again. If it is summer, listen for the cricket's song. If no crickets are singing, close your eyes and imagine the cricket's hymn. Imagine Francis talking to the cricket, holding it in his hand. Put yourself in the scene, and talk with Francis about your own pattern of worship. Discuss your feelings and questions about worship in the Church.

✧ Reflect on how you typically spend your Sundays. Are you faithful to "keeping the Sabbath holy"? If you wish to reshape your Sundays, meditate on how this might be done. Share your hopes and misgivings with God present to you.

✧ If you are not sure, find out what the liturgical season is right now. If you are unfamiliar with the season, read more about it. To go further, rediscover the liturgical calendar, the seasons of church celebrations. Perhaps you could plan realistic ways to highlight each season with home decorations, simple prayers, or family celebrations. Offer your study of the liturgical year as praise to God.

✧ Are the special moments of your life and those of your family and community celebrated? What are some of the traditions that help you celebrate them? If an important family or personal moment in your life is coming up, make plans for a celebration, thanking God for grace-filled moments.

✧ Simple reflections are wonderful worship too.
✦ Repeat aloud or silently with Francis, "I lift up my heart to you, my God."
✦ Or pray repeatedly like Francis instructed the cricket, "I praise you Creator with a joyful song." A sincere heart is a joyful song!

God's Word

"In truth I tell you once again, if two of you on earth agree to ask anything at all, it will be granted to you by my Father in heaven. For where two or three meet in my name, I am there among them." (Matthew 18:19–20)

And here are some more of my reflections:
    yes, I am as full as the moon at the full!
Listen to me, devout children, and blossom
    like the rose that grows on the bank of a watercourse.
Give off a sweet smell like incense,
    flower like the lily, spread your fragrance abroad,
sing a song of praise
    blessing the Lord for all his works.
Declare the greatness of his name,
    proclaim his praise
with song and with lyre,
    and this is how you must sing his praises:
"How wonderful, the actions of the Lord!
    Whatever he orders is done at the proper time!"
                  (Ecclesiasticus 39:12–16)

Closing prayer: Wondrous God, I ask to live and pray in rhythm with the Church and the universe, joining my voice throughout the day and year with the chorus of earth and sky, singing God's praise. Amen. Alleluia!

✧ Meditation 15 ✧

Joy

Theme: The life of Jesus should fill us with wondrous joy. As Francis proclaimed, "We are minstrels of the Lord."

Opening prayer: I pray for holy joy. We are delightful in God's eyes; may I delight in God's gracious goodness to us! I pray with Francis with singing and with my heart raised in joy!

About Francis

Brother Pacifico was an early companion of Francis. Before his conversion, Pacifico had achieved fame as a master of the courtly songs which were the popular music of the time. Indeed, he was known as the King of Verse. Francis requested of Brother Pacifico that he travel about with other friars and join the singing of praises to the Lord with preaching the Gospels. For Francis, singing represented a natural expression of the spirit of his company, the spirit of joy: "What are the servants of God but his minstrels who should lift up the hearts of people and move them to spiritual joy?"

The image of Francis and his companions traveling through the towns and countrysides of Italy, singing and bursting with unrestrained joy, was surely a common one. Francis found joy in the message of the Gospel. As is always true with joy, his became contagious. Since his time, "Franciscan joy" has become an identifying mark of Francis and of those who share his spirit. (Adapted from Clissold, *The Wisdom of St. Francis,* p. 88)

Pause: Reflect on the image of joyful Francis.

Francis' Words

The God whom Francis loved was to be enjoyed. Once when Francis noticed one of the friars walking along with lowered head and a gloomy countenance, he rebuked him for such an outward display of sadness. He suggested that he keep his sorrow between himself and God and to pray for a restoration of his soul to the joy of God's healing. "But in front of me and others show yourself as always having joy; for it is not fitting for a servant of God to show sadness outwardly, or to have a clouded face" (Clissold, *The Wisdom of St. Francis,* p. 67).

Reflection

Francis reminds us that God's unconditional love for us is the cause of our joy and that nothing will separate us from God's love.

Joy is an essential of life. Unlike happiness, which comes and goes like the weather, one minute bright and sunny, the next cloudy and rainy, joy wells up from the source of our life and makes living worthwhile. Joy runs deep. It is never superficial. It withstands suffering and pain. In fact, it transforms pain and suffering into compassion. Joy leads us to celebrate that in good times and bad, we belong to God.

✦ Think of the people in your life who are joyful. Take your time; don't rush. Who are they? You may need to close your eyes and bring their faces into view. Why are they joyful? How do they express joy? After you have recalled these people of joy, select one of them to talk with. Ask why she or he is so joyful; carry on a dialog with her or him, exploring the sources of joy, especially the role of Jesus.

✧ After the angel of God announced to Mary that she would be the mother of the Messiah, she visited her aging cousin to share her joy. Elizabeth greeted Mary with an outburst of her own enthusiastic joy, for she too was with child: "The child in my womb leapt with joy at the sound of your greeting." When was the last time you "jumped for joy" because you knew that God was acting lovingly in your life? If you keep a journal, review recent events recorded there to find moments of joy. If you do not keep a journal, play back past months like a movie. Recall moments of joy, times when you knew that you were loved. How did you feel toward other people? Toward God? Compose a litany of these joyful events, for example, "For the birth of my niece, thank you God for this holy joy!" or "For reconciliation with my sister, thank you, God, for this holy joy!"

✧ If you have a particular scene from the Scriptures that exemplifies joy for you, spend some time meditating on this passage. If no passage comes to mind immediately, meditate on one of these stories:
+ The risen Jesus appears to the disciples walking to Emmaus (Luke 24:13–35)
+ Jesus is gloriously transfigured (Matthew 17:1–8)
+ Pentecost (Acts 1:1–13)

✧ Read "About Francis" again. Visualize Francis telling Brother Pacifico to sing praises to God. Now imagine Francis turning to you and, with a smile, saying, "Sing! Sing to God for all that God has done for you!" Go ahead. Sing your favorite hymn of praise to God. As the old adage says, "Those who sing, pray twice!" If you cannot remember the words to your favorite hymn, hum the melody—or slowly and joyfully recite, "My spirit finds joy in you, God my Savior."

God's Word

Mary said:

> My being proclaims your greatness,
> and my spirit finds joy in you, God my Savior.
>
> For you have looked upon me, your servant, in my
> lowliness;
> all ages to come shall call me blessed.
>
> God, you who are mighty, have done great things for
> me.
> Holy is your name.
>
> Your mercy is from age to age toward those who fear
> you.
>
> You have shown might with your arm
> and confused the proud in their inmost thoughts.
>
> You have deposed the mighty from their thrones
> and raised the lowly to high places.
>
> The hungry you have given every good thing
> while the rich you have sent away empty.
>
> You have upheld Israel your servant, ever mindful of
> your mercy—
>
> even as you promised our ancestors;
> promised Abraham, Sarah, and their descendants
> forever.
> (Nancy Schreck and Maureen Leach, *Psalms Anew,* p. 16)

Closing prayer: God, you have called me to joy. You are, indeed, the source and cause of all delight. Blessed be your holy name for the gift of this world in all its splendor! Blessed be your holy name for creating me, not for sorrow and suffering, but for joy! Blessed be my life—may it burst forth in joy for you and for all those whom I meet! Amen. Alleluia!

JOY

✧ Acknowledgments ✧

The psalms quoted in this book are from *Psalms Anew,* compiled by Nancy Schreck and Maureen Leach (Winona, MN: Saint Mary's Press, 1986). Used by permission of the publisher. All rights reserved.

All other scriptural quotations used in this book are from The New Jerusalem Bible. Copyright © 1985 by Darton, Longman & Todd, Ltd., London, and Doubleday, a division of Random House, Inc. Reprinted by permission of the publishers.

The excerpts on pages 27, 35, 36, 40, 41, 51–52, 55, 56, 70–71, 77–78, and 99–100 are from *The Wisdom of St. Francis and His Companions,* by Stephen Clissold (New York: New Directions Publishing Corporation, 1979), pages 30–31, 72, 70–71, 32, 31–32, 53, 73, 78, 59–60, 49–50 and 63, and 88 and 67 respectively. Copyright © 1978 by Stephen Clissold. Reprinted by permission of the New Directions Publishing Corp.

The excerpts on pages 27, 46, 66, and 71–72 are from *Francis and Clare: The Complete Works,* translation and introduction by Regis J. Armstrong, OFM Cap., and Ignatius C. Brady, OFM, preface by John Vaughn, OFM, (Mahwah, NJ: Paulist Press, 1982), pages 30, 105 and 115, 28, 38–39, and 115 respectively. From the Classics of Western Spirituality series. Copyright © 1982 by the Missionary Society of St. Paul the Apostle in the State of New York and Society for Promoting Christian Knowledge. Paulist Press, Inc., NY/Mahwah, N.J. www.paulistpress.com. Used by permission of Paulist Press.

The excerpts on pages 31–32 and 44–46 are from *Brother Francis,* edited by Lawrence Cunningham (New York: Harper & Row Publishers, Inc., 1975), pages 128–129 and 73–75 respectively. Copyright © 1972 by Lawrence Cunningham. Used with permission of HarperCollins Publishers, Inc.

✧ For Further Reading ✧

Chesterton, G. K. *St. Francis of Assisi.* Garden City, NY: Double-day Image Books, 1924.

Clissold, Stephen, ed. *The Wisdom of St. Francis and His Companions.* New York: New Directions, 1978.

Cunningham, Lawrence, ed. *Brother Francis: An Anthology of Writings by and About St. Francis of Assisi.* New York: Harper and Row Family Library, 1972.

Fortini, Arnaldo. *Francis of Assisi.* Trans. Helen Moak. New York: The Crossroad Publishing Company, 1980.

Francis of Assisi and Clare of Assisi. *Francis and Clare: The Complete Works.* Trans. Regis J. Armstrong and Ignatius C. Brady. New York: Paulist Press, 1982.

Habig, Marion A., ed. *St. Francis of Assisi: Writings and Early Biographies.* Chicago: Franciscan Herald Press, 1973.

Reynolds, E. E. *The Life of Saint Francis of Assisi.* Wheathampstead, UK: Anthony Clarke, 1975.